P9-EMH-194

The Lie

Evolution

Kenneth A. Ham

Master
Books

Sixteenth printing: January 1998

ISBN: 0-89051-158-6

Front cover photo: Rockafellow Photography,
                     Springfield, MO

Cover: Janell Robertson

Interior illustrations: Steve Cardno

Scripture taken from the New International Version, copyright 1984 by the International Bible Society. Used by permission of Zondervan Bible Publishers.

Printed in the United States of America.

DEDICATION

This book is dedicated to three special people without whom this publication would not have been possible:

To my mother and late father for their stand on the Scriptures and their insistence on purity of doctrine and an uncompromising acceptance of God's Word and the principles therein, applied to every area of life. This has equipped me so that a higher authority (the Lord) could call me into full-time service for Him. I thank God for this Christian training and my parents' stand on the infallible Word of God.

To my dear wife Mally, who has truly been one with me in all aspects of our married life and in our participation in the Creation ministry. Her sincere Christian dedication and devotion in regard to my involvement in this vital ministry can be summed up by the words of Ruth, in Ruth 1:16, "For whither thou goest, I will go; and where thou lodgest, I will lodge." Her special God-given abilities and her love for children have been a real blessing to our five dear children and have enabled me to be absent at times to proclaim the message of God as Creator to millions of people in various parts of the world.

ABOUT THE AUTHOR

Kenneth A. Ham, B.App.Sc., Dip.Ed., is the director and founder of Answers in Genesis in the United States and the Creation Science Foundation ministry in Australia. His background as a biology teacher in the public school system has aided him in comprehending the most complex scientific implications of the creation/evolution debate.

Ken has taught in thousands of churches, schools, universities, colleges, and has appeared on numerous radio and TV broadcasts. He hosts a daily radio program called "Answers . . . with Ken Ham." His special ministry is to apply the relevance of the creation/evolution issue to the life of the average Christian. A skilled communicator with a keen sense of humor and captivating experiences, Ken has the gift of being able to take complex and confusing philosophies and make them understandable to the average person.

Ken is the author of *A is for Adam* (a children's rhyme book) and is the co-author of *The Answers Book*. Ken can be contacted in the USA through:

Answers in Genesis
P.O. Box 6330 ● Florence, KY 41022-6330 U.S.A.
(606) 647-2900 ● FAX: (606) 371-4448

or in Australia through:

Creation Science Foundation
P.O. Box 6302
Acacia Ridge DC, QLD 4110 ● Australia
Phone: (07) 273 7650 ● FAX: (07) 273 7672
International: +617 3273 7672 ● FAX: 617 3273 7672

CONTENTS

There is a war in society—Christianity versus humanism. Too few realize that the essence of the conflict lies firmly at the foundational level—creation versus evolution—Because it is beneficial in waging successful warfare first to identify the field, this chapter establishes the true nature of the battlefront.

The media and the public education system tell us that "creation" cannot be taught in schools because it is religion, while "evolution" is science. It is easy to grasp the basic tenets of science and quickly come to the conclusion that evolution is really a religion.

Creation and evolution are equally scientific and equally religious. The controversy is *not* religion versus science, but the science of one religion versus the science of another religion.

practices, and worse. Increase in the popularity of evolution has gone hand-in-hand with the increase in popularity of these social issues. While evolution is not to blame for the social ills of society, it has become the justification for lending respectability to such social attitudes. The ultimate cause of these problems is the rejection of God as Creator.

Chapter Nine—Evangelism In A Pagan World

Creation evangelism may be a new term to many, but it is a Biblical method. Paul used it with great success. Creation evangelism is a tool the church needs to use to restore the right foundations in order to present the whole Gospel message. Evolution is one of the biggest barriers to today's people being receptive to the Gospel of Jesus Christ. Creation evangelism is a powerful method that removes these barriers and opens people's hearts and minds to the Gospel.

Chapter Ten—Wake Up, Shepherds!

A plea to pastors and other religious leaders to see the importance of the creation/evolution issue. It is not a side issue. Many religious leaders don't realize the true nature of the creation/evolution controversy because they have been hoodwinked into thinking that what they have been led to believe is true science. The church is suffering greatly because many have compromised with evolution.

Chapter Eleven—Creation, Flood and Coming Fire

A message and warning from II Peter 3 concerning the rejection in the last days of the belief in God as Creator. This should be a real warning to all of the importance of origins. The prophecy in II Peter 3 concerning the last days is being fulfilled before our very eyes.

Resources

Appendices

The material in the appendices is meant to provide detailed answers on the questions people have concerning the creation/evolution issue.

ACKNOWLEDGEMENTS

As this book is a culmination of ten years experience in the creation ministry based in Australia, it is not an easy task to recall all those who have helped and influenced me along the way.

When we inaugurated the Creation Science Foundation ministry in Australia, we certainly did not realize the far-reaching effects this ministry would have in different parts of the world. My colleagues, Professor John Rendle-Short, Dr. John Osgood, Dr. Andrew Snelling, and Dr. Steve Gustafson will recognize snippets of their research and lectures that have benefited me greatly over the years.

I would also like to sincerely thank Mr. W.F.G. Gadsby, Rev. P. Gadsby, Mr. Robert Doolan, and Dr. Len Morris for editing and reviewing the manuscript. My heartfelt thanks also to my special friend Dr. Carl Wieland who, in spite of massive injuries received in a horrendous car accident, worked with me in editing the manuscript a number of times. Many of his suggestions have been incorporated in this book to give it a polish I would not have been able to obtain by myself.

Special thanks must also be given to my two devoted secretaries: to Carol Van Luyn for the many hours spent typing and retyping the manuscript; to Margaret Buchanan for her talented editorial skills and patience as she painstakingly worked for literally hundreds of hours in helping me put the manuscript together.

I would like to thank my good friend and Creation Science Foundation artist Steve Cardno for the tireless expenditure of his God-given talents to produce the illustrations throughout this book. These and many other illustrations are reproduced on overhead transparencies and are used in my teaching ministry with great effectiveness.

The name of Dr. Gary Parker appears on occasions throughout

this book. Dr. Parker is a well known creationist speaker and author. I have had the privilege of appearing with him on various platforms in Australia and the United States. The many experiences shared together have contributed greatly to this book.

Lastly, I would like to sincerely thank Dr. Henry Morris of the Institute for Creation Research. His books, particularly *The Genesis Record*, have had a profound influence on my life. In this regard, I feel rather like the apprentice—and no doubt the master will recognize some of his work in the pages of this book. And to all my friends and colleagues who have been towers of strength to me over the past years—thank you.

FOREWORD

Perhaps you have not been notably successful in winning friends and acquaintances to the life-changing belief in God and His Son, Jesus Christ. You might have wondered why the Christian church in general seems to be losing ground in its battle with the evils of the secular world. Not only does this book identify the reason for such problems, but it also offers an effective solution. When you read Ken Ham's logical analysis of the situation and the straightforward way in which he proposes to correct it, you will likely say, "Why didn't I think of that?"

At an ever-accelerating pace, society is putting its stamp of approval on practices that just several decades ago were not only frowned upon, but were outright illegal. Whereas once the Christian church had a significant impact on society, today almost every vestige of our Christian heritage is being eradicated. After spreading like wildfire, from a tiny handful of believers to the four corners of the world, Christianity today is in retreat at an even more rapid rate than that by which it spread.

There must be a root cause for this reversal that the Christian church is overlooking—a fundamental flaw in our approach. Why did Christians once exert influence on both social customs and laws of government, but today they are finding that even in the United States, the so-called land of the free with a constitution that guarantees the free exercise of religion, their rights are being flagrantly violated?

Ken Ham gets to the bottom of the problem in this book. He shows how we have been simply fighting the symptoms and overlooking the root cause. Why have we not been able to convince the world of the evils of abortion, divorce, homosexuality, pornography, and drugs? Mr. Ham has identified the real crux of the matter. The cause is so subtle that even most of the large religious denominations have been deceived and have failed to recognize it.

With public education and even seminaries teaching that evolution, as well as the law of gravity, is a scientific fact, students have decided that there must be a naturalistic explanation for everything, so they forgot all about God. Anyway, they knew that His Ten Commandments put a crimp on their sexual lifestyles, so they were quite eager to escape from such constraints. They adopted the new morality: if it feels good, do anything you can get away with without being caught.

If there is no Creator, there is no purpose in life. There is thus no one watching over us to whom we must someday have to account for our actions. So, we come to the root of society's problems. When God the Creator is removed from the picture, there are no absolutes; there is a loss of respect for law and absolute principles, and man is set adrift in a purposeless universe, guided only by his fickle passions and the situation of the moment.

Mr. Ham shows that Genesis, in particular, is a dependable account of actual events that are supported by solid scientific evidence. Furthermore, he shows how the questioning of this foundational book of the Bible, even by many Christians, has led to the degeneration of society so that the only moral codes it accepts are based upon "survival of the fittest," "do your own thing," and "if it feels good, do it." There are no moral absolutes.

This book is must reading for all Christians. It gives them much needed answers to the common questions of the unbeliever and advice for parents who must prepare their children to face a rebellious secular world. Mr. Ham calls upon a wealth of experience in answering questions during years of lectures throughout both America and Australia.

Luther D. Sunderland
January, 1987
Author of *Darwin's Enigma: Fossils and Other Problems*

INTRODUCTION

I was reared in a Christian home where the Bible was totally accepted as the infallible, inerrant Word of God that provided the basis for the principles to be applied in every area of life. I recognized the conflict when, as a high school student, I was taught the theory of evolution. If Genesis was not literally true, then what part of the Bible could I trust?

My parents knew that evolution was wrong, because it was obvious from Genesis that God had given us the details of the creation of the world. These details were important foundational truths for the rest of Christianity. At that time, the current wealth of materials on the creation/evolution issue produced, for instance, by the Institute for Creation Research were not available. I recall going to my local minister and asking him what to do about the problem. He told me to accept evolution but then add it to the Bible so that God used evolution to bring all forms of life into being. This was an unsatisfactory solution to the problem. If God did not mean what He said in Genesis, then how could one trust Him in the rest of the Scriptures?

I went through my science degree and my teacher training year pigeon-holing this problem, regurgitating to the lecturers what they told me concerning evolution. I did not know from a scientific perspective why I did not believe in evolution—but I knew from a Biblical perspective it had to be wrong or my faith was in trouble.

Just before I received my first teaching appointment, the associate director of a teachers' college in Australia, Mr. Godron Jones (a member of the church I was attending) gave me a small book outlining some of the problems with evolution. He also told me of books that were becoming available on this topic—books authored by such people as Dr. Henry Morris. I searched the bookshops to try to collect as much of this material as possible. *The Genesis Flood* by Morris and Whitcomb was one of the first books I read on the subject. When I realized there were easy answers to this creation/evolution dilemma, there came a real burden from the Lord to go out and share this information with others. I could not understand why the Church had not made people aware of this information which really helped restore my faith in the Scriptures.

Understanding the foundational nature of the book of Genesis to all Christian doctrine was a real awakening. This book is the result of a series of messages developed so that Christians could understand the significance and relevance of Genesis and the real nature of the creation/evolution issue. Over and over again, people have come and said that they had never realized the importance of Genesis—in fact, for many of them it meant a complete revival of their faith. It is gratifying to know that many of these people are still committed supporters of the creation ministries.

This book deals with the relevance of a literal Genesis. I pray that it will challenge mind and heart in pastor, layperson, scholar and student alike.

CHAPTER 1

Christianity is Under Attack

After the lecture, a young man approached me—"What you said
. . . it's suddenly like a light bulb lighting up in my head!" A young
lady standing nearby stated, "I realized today that my understanding
of Christianity was like starting in the middle of a movie—**you** took
me back to the beginning—now I understand what it is all about."
A middle-aged man approached, "This information is like a key. It
not only unlocks the reason as to why we have problems in society
today—it's the key to knowing how to be much more effective in
witnessing for Jesus Christ . . . . Thank you."

These are challenging days. On the whole, society is becoming more
anti-Christian. We are seeing steady increases in homosexuality, support
for abortion on demand, unwillingness to obey authorities, unwillingness
to work, marriage being abandoned, clothing being abandoned, an
increase in pornography, and an increase in lawlessness, to name but
a few areas. Christians are fighting for their freedom even in so-called
"Christian" nations.

What has happened in society to bring about these changes? Why
is it that many people are cynical when you talk about Christ and
seem to be closed to the Gospel? There must be some foundational
reason for this change. In this book we will discover the basic reasons
why modern society has turned away from Christ. More importantly,
there will be outlined for you a Biblical (and hence successful) way
to reclaim lives for our Savior.

Years ago, our society was based on Christian absolutes. People knew what was right and what was wrong. Behaviors such as sexual deviancy, easy divorce, public lawlessness, abortion on demand, pornography and public nudity were considered to be wrong. Varying punishments for offenders were meted out by society. Value judgments were basically built on Biblical principles (for example, The Ten Commandments). Most people accepted or respected a belief in God.

Recently more and more people have rejected the God of the Bible. As belief in God has been abandoned, people have questioned the basis of the society in which they live. For instance, if there is no God, then why should they obey the Ten Commandments? Why should anyone say that homosexuality is wrong? Why should not women be allowed to have abortions whenever they desire? Once people eliminated God from their consciences, they set about to change any laws based on Christian absolutes that held God as Creator (and thus Owner) of everything.

Christian absolutes have been diluted or removed as the basis of society and replaced with a world view that says, "We do not have to accept that the Christian way of doing things (basing our world and life view on Biblical principles) is the only way; we must tolerate all religious beliefs and ways of life." However, this "tolerance" really means an *intolerance of the absolutes of Christianity*. This false idea of tolerance has subtly undermined Christianity, and most Christians have not recognized what was really happening. Many Christians have been deceived into believing they have no right to impose their views on society. We are told, for instance, that anti-abortionists have no business impressing their particular bias on society. Have you ever heard anyone say this about the pro-abortion groups? The result is one bias being imposed on society by the pro-abortionists—*legalized abortion* on demand! No matter what you do, you cannot avoid the fact that a view is being imposed on someone by someone. There is no such thing as neutrality, although many Christians become ensnared in the trap of believing there is.

It is like the many theological and Bible colleges that say, "We do not take a dogmatic stand on Genesis. We tolerate all views." But what happens when someone comes along and says, "Will you allow the view that says you *must* take Genesis literally?" "Oh, no!" they say, "We cannot allow that view because we tolerate all views!" In reality, they have taken a dogmatic stand to teach a dogmatic view to their students—a view that you do not have to take Genesis literally if you do not want to do so.

At one lecture I gave, a person said in an angry tone, "This is not fair, you are insisting that we take Genesis literally, that God actually took six days, that evolution is not true and that there really was a world-wide flood. You are being intolerant of other people's views. You must show tolerance for people such as I who believe God used evolution and that Genesis is only symbolic." I then asked, "Well, what do you want me to do?" The person replied, "You must allow other views and be tolerant of opinions different to yours." "Well," I said, "My view is that the literal interpretation of Genesis is the right view. All other views concerning Genesis are wrong. Will you tolerate my view?" The person looked shocked, and he hesitated. I could almost hear him thinking, "If I say yes, then I've allowed him to say you can't have another view such as mine; if I say no, then I've obviously been intolerant of his view—what do I do?" He then looked at me and said, "That's semantics!" What he really meant was that he had lost the argument and did not want to admit his intolerance of my position. The fact is, he had taken a dogmatic, closed-minded position.

Occasionally people are upset when dogmatic statements are made. They say, "You cannot be dogmatic like that." This in itself is a dogmatic statement. **Many think that some people are dogmatic and others are not. It is not a matter of whether you are dogmatic or not, but of which dogma is the best dogma with which to be dogmatized!**

At one time, a group called "Toleration" began. They were insisting on a tolerance of all religious ways, beliefs and customs. They said that we had to stop intolerance in society. In their promotional leaflet explaining their viewpoint, it was interesting that they listed all the things they were against. And most of the things of which they were intolerant were related to Christianity. What they really meant was that they wanted a tolerance of anything in society, *except Christianity*!

The idea of open-mindedness comes from the notion that there is no such thing as absolute truth, or that truth cannot be absolutely known. Some say, "There are no absolutes." Ironically, this premise has become their one absolute. Such ideas are derived from an anti-Biblical philosophy which holds that everything is relative.

Christian absolutes—those truths and standards of Scripture which cannot be altered—are becoming less and less tolerated in society. Eventually this must result in the outlawing of Christianity. When Christian absolutes were the basis of society, immoral activities such as homosexual or lesbian lifestyle and pornography were outlawed. There has been a fundamental shift. Our society is now based on a relative morality: that is, a person can do what he likes and is answerable to no one but himself as long as the majority of people can be persuaded that their interests are not being threatened. This results in society's being told that no one can say anything against those who choose to be sexual deviants, go naked publicly or do whatever they want (within the limits of the law, which is also changing to become more "tolerant" of people's actions).

God's absolutes dictate that there are rules by which we must abide. Christianity cannot co-exist in a world community with relative morality as its basis. One or the other will yield. There are two world views with two totally different belief systems clashing in our society. The real war being waged is a great spiritual war. Sadly, today many Christians fail to win the war because they fail to recognize the nature of the battle.

It is my contention that this spiritual conflict is rooted in the issue of origins (creation/evolution). Although the thought may sound strange or new to the reader, Biblically and logically this issue is central in the battle for men's souls.

Most people have the wrong idea about what the creation/evolution question involves. Instead of perceiving the real issue, they have been deceived into believing that evolution is science. It is not a science at all (refer to Chapter 2). It is a belief system about the past. We do not have access to the past. We only have the present. All the fossils, all the living animals and plants, our planet, the universe— everything exists in the present. We cannot directly test the past using the scientific method (which involves repeating things and watching them happen) since all evidence that we have is in the present.

It is important to understand that special creation, by definition, is also a belief about the past. The difference is that creationists base their understanding of creation upon a book which claims to be the *Word of the One who was there*, who knows everything there is to know about everything, and who tells us what happened. Evolution

4 COMMONLY BELIEVED FACTS ABOUT THE SCIENTIST IN THE WHITE COAT:

1. He is unbiased
2. He is objective
3. He is infallible
4. He wears a white coat

"THE MAN IN THE WHITE COAT" —entirely unbiased and completely objective in his search for scientific truth.

AN EXAMPLE OF A REAL SCIENTIST !

* NOTE BOOKS AND AWARDS

4 TRUTHS ABOUT SCIENTISTS:
1. He is BIASED (look at his books).
2. He is NOT OBJECTIVE !
3. He is HUMAN !
4. He seldom wears a WHITE COAT !

comes from the words of men who *were not there* and who do not claim to be omniscient. This whole issue revolves around whether we believe the words of God who was there, or the words of fallible humans (no matter how qualified) who were not there.

It is astonishing in this so-called "scientific age" that so few people know what science really is or how it works. Many think of scientists as unbiased people in white laboratory coats objectively searching for the truth. However, scientists come in two basic forms, male and female, and they are just like you and me. They have beliefs and biases. A bias determines what you do with the evidence, especially the way in which you decide that certain evidence is more relevant or important than other evidence. Scientists are not objective truth-seekers; they are not *neutral.*

Many people misunderstand bias, thinking that some individuals are biased and some are not. Consider an atheist, for example: such a person believes there is no God. Can atheists entertain the question, "Did God create?" The answer is, "No." As soon as they even allow it as a question, they are no longer atheists. So, to an atheist scientist looking at the fossils and the world around him, it would not matter what evidence he were to find. It could have nothing to do with Biblical events, such as Noah's Flood. Even if he found a big boat on the top of Mount Ararat he could never allow that evidence to support the claims of the Bible regarding Noah's Ark. As soon as he did, he would have abandoned his atheistic religious framework. An atheist is one hundred percent biased. This should be kept in mind whenever one reads a textbook or sees a television program produced by an atheist.

I have seen many examples of bias exhibited in various ways. I was on a talk-back radio show in Denver, Colorado, and the radio announcer said I had seven minutes to give the evidence for creation. He would just sit back and listen. So I went into detail about what the Bible says concerning Noah's Flood, the Tower of Babel, and other related topics. I explained how evidence from various cultures and from the fossil record supported what the Bible said. Various other aspects of creation were explored to demonstrate the truth of the Bible. At the end of the seven minutes the announcer made this comment on the air, "Well, I didn't hear any evidence for creation at all; so much for that!" Of course, what he meant was that he was not prepared to accept the evidence that I had given him because he wanted to hold on to his own bias: agnosticism. An agnostic is one hundred percent biased. He believes one cannot know anything for sure, so, no matter how much evidence he hears, he can still say, "I do not know." As soon as he knows, he has stopped being an agnostic. From a Biblical perspective, Romans 1 teaches that the evidence for creation is all around us and, therefore, anyone who does not believe in the Creator and Savior is condemned. It is also important to recognize that one does not have to see the Creator to recognize the fact of special creation. Just because one cannot see the architect and builder who designed and constructed a house does not mean that there was not an intelligent designer behind it.

But what about a revelationist, that is, a person who believes that the God of history has revealed the truth about Himself by means of a book? (A book which claims over three thousand times to be the Word of God.) Can such a person consider the opposite question, that God did **not** create? No! Because he starts with the premise that God is Creator and His word is true.

Atheists, agnostics and revelationists (and theists) hold to religious positions; and what they do with the evidence will again be determined by the assumptions (beliefs) of their religious positions. **It is not a matter of whether one is biased or not. It is really a question of which bias is the best bias with which to be biased.**

Glaring examples of bias can be seen in public education in response to the creation ministry. The following conversation, which is rather typical of students in the public school system, shows what bias is all about. After a presentation on creation, one student stated, "There is no way Noah's Ark could be true—he couldn't have fitted all the animals on board." I then asked the student, "How many animals would he have needed to have put on board?" He gave the usual reply: "I don't know, but it certainly couldn't have happened." "I then asked him how big was the ark?" Again he answered, "I don't know, but he couldn't have fitted the animals on board." In other words, here is a student who did not know how big Noah's Ark was, or how many animals God would have needed to put on board, but he has already decided it is a fairy tale that could not have happened.

At one town a keen supporter of creation ministries told how he had spoken to fellow academics at a local university concerning Noah's

Flood. They, of course, mocked and scoffed at the idea. He then mentioned that someday someone may find Noah's Ark on Mount Ararat. One fellow academic turned to him and said that even if they found a big boat that looked like Noah's Ark on top of Mount Ararat and dragged it to the main street of the city, he would still refuse to believe it. His bias was showing.

There have been many occasions where I have been able to give a convincing and logical presentation to the students. Many of them then looked to their teachers to try to make some point that could demonstrate where I was wrong. It is easy to read the expressions on the students' faces. They are saying that this all sounds convincing, but surely there must be something wrong with it because they really do not want to believe that the Bible is true. A teacher may respond by asking a question that sounds to the student as if the teacher has proven me wrong. In the students' eyes there is no way that I would be able to answer the question. Often students spontaneously break into applause (their way of rejoicing over what they think is my demise). However, it is interesting to watch their faces and see their jaws drop when I am able to give a reasonable answer to the question—they are back where they started. It is sad to see that, for many of them, they have already made up their minds and decided they really do not want to believe the Bible.

I am often asked how people change their biases. This is a good question. As a Christian, the only way I can answer is to say that in this area it has to be a work of the Holy Spirit. The Bible teaches that we either walk in light or in darkness (Acts 26:18), gather or scatter, are **for** Christ or **against** Him (Matthew 12:30). The Bible clearly declares that no person is neutral and that all do have a bias. Since it is the Holy Spirit who convicts and convinces people of the truth, it is only through the work of the Holy Spirit that our biases can change. As Christians, our job is to bring the Word of God to people in a clear and gracious way, and pray that the Spirit might use our words to open hearts and minds to Christ. I believe Christians understand bias better than others. All Christians were once lost sinners biased against God. They have seen how Jesus Christ can change their bias as He transforms their lives through the power of His Spirit.

One of the reasons why creationists have such difficulty in talking to certain evolutionists is because of the way bias has affected the way they hear what we are saying. They already have preconceived ideas about what we do and do not believe. They have prejudices about what they want to understand in regard to our scientific qualifications, and so on.

	BASIS	INFLUENCE	BIAS
ATHEISM	NO GOD EXISTS	CAN'T CONSIDER CREATION	100%
AGNOSTIC	DON'T CARE CAN'T KNOW DON'T KNOW	MUST EXCLUDE DEFINITE ROLE OF GOD OPEN?	100%
THEISM	GOD DEDUCED	NO ABSOLUTES	100%
REVEALED	GOD REVEALED TO MAN	ABSOLUTE REFERENCE POINTS	100%

There are many examples of evolutionists who have totally misunderstood or misinterpreted what creationists are saying. They hear us through their "evolutionary ears," not comprehending in the slightest the perspective from which we are coming. As creationists, we understand that God created a perfect world, man fell into sin, the world was cursed, God sent Noah's Flood as judgment, and Jesus Christ came to die and be raised from the dead to restore all things. In other words, our message is one of Creation, Fall and Redemption. However, because evolutionists are used to thinking in "uniformitarian" terms (i.e., basically the world we see today—the world of death and struggle—has gone on for millions of years), they do not understand this creationist perspective of history.

An interesting example came when Dr. Gary Parker was debating a professor from LaTrobe University in Victoria, Australia. One of the evolutionist's "refutations" of creation centered around his assertion that there were too many imperfections in the world to have been made by a Creator. This particular evolutionist would not understand, even after it was clearly presented, that the world we are looking at today is not the same world that God created because of the effects of the Fall and Flood. To understand the creation/evolution issue correctly, one must have a complete understanding of the beliefs adhered to by both creationists and evolutionists.

In another example, an evolutionist biologist said that if God made all the animals during the fifth and sixth days of creation, why don't we find parakeets and mice in the Cambrian strata alongside trilobites? Dr. Parker then explained that parakeets and mice do not live in the same environment as the trilobites. Dr. Parker explained to this scientist that the fossil record should be seen in terms of the sorting action of a world-wide flood. Because animals and plants live in different areas, they would have been trapped in sediments representative of their particular environment. Again, we see bias causing a misunderstanding that so many have of the creationist position.

The reader needs to be aware that, when we discuss creation/evolution, in both instances we are talking about beliefs, that is, religion. The controversy is not religion versus science, as the evolutionists try to make out. It is religion versus religion, the science of one religion versus the science of the other.

Evolution is a religious position that makes human opinion supreme. As we shall see, its fruits (because of rejection of the Creator and Lawgiver) are lawlessness, immorality, impurity, abortion, racism and a mocking of God. Creation is a religious position based on the Word of God, and its fruits (through God's Spirit) are love, joy, peace, patience, kindness, goodness, faithfulness, gentleness and self-control. The creation/evolution issue (is God Creator?) is the crux of the problems in our society today. It is the fundamental issue with which Christians must come to grips. The creation/evolution issue is where the battle really rages.

CHAPTER 2

Evolution is Religion

The term "evolutionist" is used extensively throughout the following chapters. In other parts of this book, we will discuss the ideas of Christians who try to marry the concepts of evolution and the Bible. However, because the majority of evolutionists are not Christians, I wish the reader to understand that the term "evolutionist" is used to mean those who believe that evolution—in the sense of time, chance and struggle for survival—rather than the God of the Bible is responsible for life.

In the official journal of the South Australian branch of the Australian Skeptics (this organization has similar aims to American humanist groups), the entire 30 pages of *The Southern Skeptic*, Volume 2 Number 5, Autumn 1985, were devoted to an attack on the creation science ministry in Australia and the United States. On the last page, we read the following: "Even if all the evidence ended up supporting whichever scientific theories best fitted Genesis, this would only show how clever the old Hebrews were in their use of common sense, or how lucky. It does not need to be explained by an unobservable God." These people who vehemently attack the creation ministry in saying we are a religious group are themselves a religious group. They have really said that even if all the evidence supported the book of Genesis they still would not believe it was an authoritative document. They are working from the premise that the Bible is not the Word of God, nor can it ever be. They believe, no matter what the evidence, that there is no God. These same people are most adamant that evolution is a fact.

Evolution is basically a religious philosophy. We in creation ministries are explaining to people that both creation and evolution are religious views of life upon which people build their particular models of philisophy, science or history. The issue, therefore, is not science versus religion, but religion versus religion (the science of one religion versus the science of another religion).

The famous evolutionist Theodosius Dobzhansky (*The American Biology Teacher*, Volume 35, Number 3, March 1973, page 129) quotes Pierre Teilhard de Chardin: "Evolution is a light which illuminates all facts, a trajectory which all lines of thought must follow." To the Christian, of course, this is a direct denial of the sayings of Jesus as quoted in John 8:12 (NIV): "I am the light of the world. Whoever follows me will never walk in darkness, but will have the light of life." In Isaiah 2:5 (NIV) we are exhorted to "walk in the light of the Lord." In verse 22 of the same chapter we read, "Stop trusting in man . . . ."

It does not take much effort to demonstrate that evolution is *not* science but *religion*. Science, of course, involves observation, using one or more of our five senses (taste, sight, smell, hearing, touch) to gain knowledge about the world and to be able to repeat the observations. Naturally, one can only observe what exists in the present. It is an easy task to understand that no scientist was present over the suggested millions of years to witness the supposed evolutionary progression of life from the simple to the complex. No living scientist was there to observe the first life forming in some primeval sea. No living scientist was there to observe the Big Bang that is supposed to have occurred 10 or 20 billion years ago, nor the supposed formation of the earth 4.5 billion years ago (or even 10,000 years ago!). No scientist was there—no human witness was there to see these events occurring. They certainly cannot be repeated today.

All the evidence a scientist has exists *only* in the present. All the fossils, the living animals and plants, the world, the universe—in fact, everything, exists *now*—in the present. The average person (including most students) is *not* taught that scientists have only the present and cannot deal directly with the past. Evolution is a belief system about the past based on the words of men who were not there, but who are trying to explain how all the evidence of the present (that is, fossils, animals and plants, etc.) originated. (Webster's Dictionary defines religion as follows: " . . . cause, principle or system of beliefs held to with ardor and faith." Surely, this is an apt description of evolution.) Evolution is a belief system—a religion!

It only takes common sense to understand that one does not dig up an "age of the dinosaurs" supposedly existing 70-200 million years ago. One digs up *dead* dinosaurs that exist *now, not* millions of years ago.

Fossil bones do not come with little labels attached telling you how old they are. Nor do fossils have photographs with them telling you what the animals looked like as they roamed the earth long ago.

FOSSILS EXIST IN THE PRESENT

When people visit a museum they are confronted by bits and pieces of bones and other fossils neatly arranged in glass cases. These are often accompanied by pictures representing an *artist's impression* of what the animals and plants could have looked like in their natural environment. Remember, no one dug up the picture, just the fossils. And these fossils exist in the present. For example, in Tasmania there

is a sandstone bed containing millions of pieces of bones, most of which are no larger than the end of your thumb. The evolutionists have placed a picture at one particular excavation so that tourists can see how the animals and plants lived in the region "millions of years ago." You can stare at those pieces of bones for as long as you like, but you will never see the picture the scientists have drawn. The picture is their story of their own preconceived bias, and that, ultimately, is all it ever can be.

When lecturing in schools and colleges, I like to ask the students what can be learned from a fossil deposit. I ask the students whether all the animals and plants contained in the deposits lived together, died together, or were buried together. I then warn them to make sure that the answer they give me is consistent with true scientific research. As they think about it, they come to realize that they do not know if the organisms lived together because they did not see it happen. They do not know if the organisms died together because they did not see that happen either. All they really know is that they are buried together because they were found together. Therefore, if you try reconstructing the environment in which the organisms lived just from what you find there, you could be making a terrible mistake. The correct use of science needs to be emphasized in our educational system.

The only way one could always be sure of arriving at the right conclusion about anything, including origins, depends upon one's knowing everything there is to know. Unless he knew that every bit of evidence was available, he could never really be sure that any of his conclusions were right. He would never know what further evidence there might be to discover and, therefore, whether this would change his conclusions. Neither could a person ever know if he had reached the point where he had all the evidence. This is a real problem for any human being—how can he ever be one hundred percent sure about anything? It is something of a dilemma, is it not? It is like watching a murder mystery on television. What happens? It is obvious. Halfway through the viewer knows who did it—the butler. Towards the end, this conclusion is still obvious. Three minutes before the end, new evidence is admitted that you did not have before, and this totally changes your conclusions. It wasn't the butler after all!

However, starting with the irrefutable evidence of the Scriptures, we are told that in God the Father and His Christ " . . . are hidden all the treasures of wisdom and knowledge" (Colossians 2:3). There is no way any human mind can know all there is to know. But we have Someone who does. This ends our dilemma. We are in no doubt that what God has revealed in His Word is truthful and accurate. He is not a man that He should lie (Numbers 23:19) about **anything**. In time, we will know more fully. He will add to our knowledge, but He will not change what His Word has already revealed.

No human being, no scientist has all the evidence. That is why scientific theories change continuously. As scientists continue to learn new things, they change their conclusions.

The story has been told of a person who went back to his university professor many years after completing his degree in Economics. He asked to look at the test questions they were now using. He was surprised to see that they were virtually the same questions he was asked when he was a student. The lecturer then said that although the questions were the same the answers now were entirely different!

I once debated with a geology professor from an American University on a radio program. He said that evolution was real science because evolutionists were prepared to continually change their theories as they found new data. He said that creation was not science because a creationist's views were set by the Bible and, therefore, were not subject to change.

I answered, "The reason scientific theories change is because we don't know everything, isn't it? We don't have all the evidence."

"Yes, that's right," he said.

I replied, "But, we will never know *everything*."

"That's true," he answered.

I then stated, "We will always continue to find new evidence."

"Quite correct," he said. I replied, "That means we can't be *sure* about *anything*."

"Right," he said.

"That means we can't be sure about evolution."

"Oh, no! Evolution is a fact," he blurted out. He was caught by his own logic. He was demonstrating how his view was determined by his bias.

Models of science are subject to change for both creationists and evolutionists. *But, the beliefs that these models are built on are not.*

The problem is that most scientists do not realize that it is the belief (or religion) of evolution that is the basis for the scientific models (the interpretations, or stories) used to attempt an explanation of the present. Evolutionists are not prepared to change their actual belief that all life can be explained by natural processes and that no God is involved (or even needed). Evolution is the religion to which they are committed. Christians need to wake up to this. **Evolution is a religion; it is not science!**

EVOLUTION IS RELIGION

CHAPTER 3

Creation is Religion

Biblical creation is the religion upon which Creator-honoring science is built (often called scientific creationism). It is based on the Word (the Bible) of the One who claims that He was there in the past (who is, in fact, outside of time). He moved men by His Spirit to write His words so that we would have an adequate basis for finding out and understanding all we need to know about God's creation.

We need to define in detail what we mean by the creationist view. This consists of basically a threefold view of history—a perfect creation, corrupted by sin, to be restored by Jesus Christ. A summary of these concepts is as follows:

1. In six days God created the heavens, the earth and all that is in them from nothing—each part is designed to work with all the others in perfect harmony. When God completed his work of creation, He called it all "very good." There was no death. People and animals were all vegetarian, and the earth appears to have had a mild climate from pole to pole, an ideal underground nutrient-rich watering system, and no storms.

2. However, we no longer live in the world God originally created. Because our first parents placed human opinion above God's word (as we continue to do), struggle and death entered the world and God cursed the creation. Charles Darwin called this struggle to the death "natural selection" and offered his theory as a substitute for the Creator. Evolutionists later added accidental changes in heredity (mutations) to their theory. But death and accident do not create: instead they bring disease, defects, death and decay into the world God created.

After mankind's sin and rebellion (the Fall) the earth became so filled with violence and corruption that God destroyed that world with a flood and gave it a fresh start with Noah, his family and the animals in the ark. Fossils—billions of dead things buried in rock layers which were laid down by water all over the earth — remind us of God's judgment on sin.

3. After the Flood, we find that the earth is again filled with violence, corruption and death because of human sin–putting man's opinion above God's Word. Christ came to heal and restore, and by his death and resurrection, He conquered death. We may be born again into eternal life as new creations in Christ, Thus as surely as God created the world and judged the world with the Flood, our ungodly world will be destroyed by fire. For those who trust in Jesus, however, there awaits eternal life in the new heavens and new earth. There will be no more corruption because God's curse will have been removed.

The Bible claims that God knows everything. He has all knowledge. If this is true, then the Bible is the word of Someone who knows everything there is to know. If we want to come to right conclusions about anything, the only sure way would be to start with the word of the One who has absolute knowledge. **We Christians must build all of our thinking in every area on the Bible. We must start with God's Word, not the word of finite, fallible man. We must judge what people say on the basis of what God's Word says—not the other way around.**

At one seminar, I stated that we must build all of our thinking upon God's Word. That must be our starting point. One minister, in a rather irate manner, made the comment that he should be able to go to the Bible to find out how to fix his car. Obviously, he did not understand that the principles that govern our thinking in every area must come from the Scriptures. These principles are immutable. The Bible certainly does not contain the details as to how to fix a car. On the other hand, modern science, which enabled the development of the car, arose when people began to base their science upon the Bible. Therefore, this machine runs according to the laws which God made. We should be able to investigate these laws and apply them in different areas. No informed evolutionist would question the fact that modern science arose from a Biblical foundation. In other words, what we believe and how we think depends upon the basis with which

we start. The Bible contains the very foundational principles and details necessary to develop correct thinking in every area.

Unfortunately, too many people have started with the word of men and then judged what the Bible states. What an arrogant position this is! We cannot tell God what He should say. We must be prepared to come totally under His authority and listen to what He says to us. Yes, creation is religion, but it is based on revelation from the all-knowing Creator. Evolution is religion, but it is *not* based on revelation from God. Instead it is based on the words of men who were not there—men who (by their own admission) do not know everything. And these men, the Bible informs us, are biased against God and His Word.

If the Bible is not the infallible word of the One who knows everything, then we have exactly nothing. We can never be sure about anything. What then is truth: my word, your word, or someone else's word?

In fact, how do you determine what truth is or how to search for it?

I recall a seminar where a young man stated, "I can't believe in creation. I believe in the Big Bang. We are just products of chance and random processes. There is no God. What do you say to that?" I replied, "Well, if you are a product of chance, your brain is also a product of chance. Therefore, the thought patterns that determine your logic are also products of chance. If your logic is the result of chance processes, you can't be sure it evolved properly. You can't be sure you're even asking the right question because you can't trust your own logic." He was dumbfounded. Afterwards he came up and asked for the best books on the subject and said he would have to seriously think this through. He had begun to realize that, without an absolute (God), he had nothing.

Christians have the Bible which claims to be the Word of God. We can also take what the Bible says and see if the evidence of the present does fit. If we take the book of Genesis, which claims to be the account of our origins and history, we can see what it says concerning how the world was created and what subsequently happened. We can decide what we would expect to find if the Bible is true (this is our scientific model relating to creation). Then we can look at the world to see if the evidence is there (that is, investigate the present—all the evidence we have—to see if it fits with our model).

For example, we are told that God created living things in distinct kinds, or groups. We can postulate, therefore, that animals and plants should be found in kinds—that one kind cannot change into another. In fact, this is exactly what we do find (in living as well as fossil organisms).

Genesis tells us that, because of wickedness, God judged the world with a world-wide flood. If this is true, what sort of evidence would we find? We could expect that we would find billions of dead things (fossils) buried in rock layers, laid down by water and catastrophic processes over most of the earth. This is exactly what we observe.

In Genesis 11, we read of events that occurred at the Tower of Babel. Again, we can ask the question: If this event really happened, what evidence would we expect to find? Does the evidence from the cultures throughout the world fit with this?

Again, the answer is overwhelmingly "Yes." All humans can interbreed and produce fertile offspring—we are all the same kind. All humans have the same color (genetics tells us it's differing shades of the one color). If all humans had the same ancestor, Noah (and ultimately Adam), then all cultures have developed since Noah's Flood and the division at the Tower of Babel.

Evolutionists talk about the different races of people in the world today. The term "races" can be used in various ways depending upon the definition you accept. Sadly, evolutionists have used the term in the sense that some groups of humans have not evolved as far as others. When they use the word "races" they are really talking about different levels of human beings dependent upon the point to which they have evolved. Due to evolutionary teaching through the educational system and the media, many in the general public tend to think of the term "races" as applied to the human race in an evolutionary sense. Because of this situation, it is probably better for Christians to talk about one race in regard to humans, not different races. "God hath made of one blood all nations of men for to dwell on all the face of the earth, and hath determined the times before appointed, and the bounds of their habitation" (Acts 17:26, KJV).

It is known that nearly every culture in the world has stories or legends from which one could almost write the book of Genesis. Most cultures have a story about a world-wide flood similar to Noah's Flood. Creation legends—not dissimilar to the account in Genesis regarding the creation of woman, the entrance of death and the original man and animals being vegetarian (Genesis 1:29, 30)—abound in cultures around the world. This is powerful evidence that these stories have been handed down generation after generation. The true accounts are in the Bible, but the similarities in cultures around the world are not what you would expect from the viewpoint of an evolutionary belief system.

I recall being taught that the reason the Babylonians (and others) had stories similar to Genesis was because the Jews had borrowed myths of Babylonian origin to include with their writings. However, when this idea is closely investigated, we find that the Babylonian stories are rather grotesque and quite unbelievable in almost every aspect. For instance, Babylonian stories concerning the Flood have gods cutting each other in half and water spewing out. When you read the Biblical account of the Flood, it is certainly the more reasonable. When one thinks about it, stories handed down generation after generation that are not carefully preserved—particularly if they are handed down by word of mouth—do not improve with age. The truth is lost and the stories degenerate markedly. The Biblical records have been handed down in written form, carefully preserved by the superintendency of God and have not been corrupted. The Babylonian stories, which only reflect the true record in the Bible, are the ones that have become corrupted, due to the limitations of human fallibility.

Thus, starting with the Bible and working from this foundation, the evidence of the present should fit. And it does, confirming our faith that the Bible really is the Word of God. (A number of books that detail the scientific evidence in support of the Bible are listed at the end of this book.) However, this *proves* nothing scientifically, because, in relation to the past, nothing can be proven. Neither creation **nor** evolution can be proven scientifically.

Both creation and evolution are belief systems that result in different scientific models and totally different interpretations of the evidence. This is not to say that the creationist will always have exactly the right explanation about every fact. Because the creationist does not have all available data, there will be many things that may not be able to be explained in specific terms, but nonetheless, all facts should fit into the framework as set by the Biblical record.

At one church, a scientist (in a very vocal manner) stood and told the congregation not to believe what I had said. He informed them that, as a scientist, he could show them that what had been said concerning Noah's Flood and creation was wrong. Science, in his words, had proven the Bible to be wrong. Since he had stated publicly that he was a Christian, I asked him if he believed there was a person in history called Noah. He said that he did believe this. I asked him why. He told me that it was because he had read it in the Bible. I asked him if he believed that there had been a world-wide flood. His answer was no. I asked him why he did not believe there was a world-wide flood. He then went on to say it was obvious from science that there could not have been a world-wide flood—that science had proven the Bible wrong. I asked him how he could trust the Bible when it talked about Noah if he could not trust the Bible when it actually talked about Noah's Flood. I also suggested that the particular evidence he was using to say there could not have been a world-wide

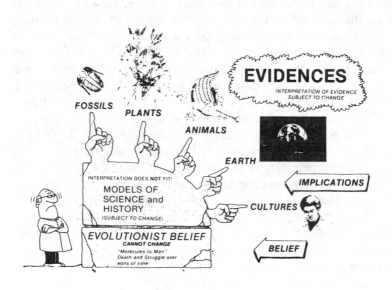

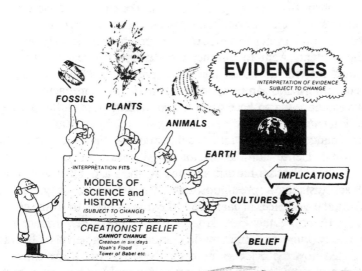

flood might be interpreted in other ways. That is, because we do not have all the evidence or know all the assumptions involved in many of the techniques used for dating the earth, etc., was it not possible that his interpretations could be wrong and the Bible could be right after all? He admitted that he did not know everything and it was possible there were assumptions behind some of the scientific methods to which he was referring. This additional information could totally change his conclusions. He admitted this was a possibility, but then he went on to say that he could not believe the Bible in all areas (e.g., Noah's Flood) until science had proven it. Again, there was a problem in understanding what science is all about and the fact that science cannot prove anything in relation to the past. I accepted the Bible as the Word of God and therefore interpreted the evidence on that basis. He was accepting the Bible as containing the Word of God but subject to proof by science. Of course, if you hold to this latter approach, **as scientists make new discoveries and their theories change all the time, your attitude towards the Bible must continually change, too—you can never be sure of anything.**

In the public school system I tried to ensure that my students were taught a correct understanding of science and how to think logically. However, when first teaching creation in the public schools, my approach was different. I would show the students the problems with evolution and how evidence supported the creationist view. However, when the students went to another class where the teacher was an evolutionist, the teacher would just reinterpret the evidence for them. I had been using what can be called an *evidentialist* approach—trying to use the evidence to convince students that it showed evolution wrong and creation true.

I then changed methods and taught students the true nature of science—what science can and cannot do. We looked in detail at the limitations that scientists have in relation to the past. They were told that all scientists have presuppositions (beliefs) which they use in interpreting the evidence. I shared with them my beliefs from the Bible concerning Creation, the Fall, Noah's Flood and other topics, and how one may build scientific models upon this framework. It was demonstrated how the evidence consistently fitted within the creation framework and not within that of the evolutionists. I had begun teaching from what could be called a "presuppositionalist" approach. The difference was astounding. When students went to the other classes and their teachers tried to reinterpret the evidence, the students were able to identify for the teachers the assumptions behind what the teachers were saying. The students recognized that it was a teacher's belief system that determined the way in which he looked at the evidence. The question of origins was outside of direct scientific proof.

This so perplexed some teachers that, on one occasion, a young teacher came to me and abrasively stated that I had destroyed her credibility with the students. She had taught her students that coal formed in swamps over millions of years. I had taught the students that there were different theories as to how coal could be formed. Since this teacher had not indicated the limitation of science and had taught her swamp theory of coal as fact, her credibility was undermined in the eyes of the students. The reason she was so angry was that she had absolutely no comeback and knew it. So did the students.

I would appeal to any who have the opportunity to teach in the area of creation/evolution to research carefully their method of teaching. Ensure that the students understand the whole philosophical area, that is, the presuppositions and assumptions involved. Not only will students understand the issues better but they will also become better scientists and thinkers as a result.

Another exciting result of this presuppositional approach emphasizing the limitations of science, is the questions students ask at the end of such a program. When using the evidentialist approach, the questions students asked would be on topics such as, "What about Carbon 14 dating?" "Haven't scientists proved fossils are millions of years old?" "Surely given enough time anything can happen." However, using the presuppositional approach (which brings the issues to the fundamental belief level), it was exciting to see a dramatic change in the nature of questions asked: "Where did God come from?" "How do you know the Bible can be trusted and is true?" "Who wrote the Bible?" "Why is Christianity better than Buddhism?" The students started to see the real issue. It was really a conflict of beliefs. The results of this approach have been astounding. Many, many students have listened to the claims of Christ and have shown real interest in Christianity with a number of conversions as a result.

This method works not only for public school students but for Christian school students as well. It is also an important method for the general public. One of the things they recognize is that creationists and evolutionists all have the same facts. Therefore, what we are really talking about are different interpretations of these same facts. They begin to see the real argument: two religions in conflict. Evidence is important (which is why creationists do intensive research), but the method used to present the evidence is vital to the success of the presentation.

After giving a lecture to a class at a Christian college in Kansas, using material similar to that discussed already (plus additional scientific evidences), a student stated in front of the rest of the class, "What you have said sounds logical and very convincing in regard to accepting Genesis as truth. But, you must be wrong, because my geology professor here at the college believes in evolution and would totally disagree with you. If he were here now, I'm sure he could tell me where you are wrong, even if I can't see it at the moment." I replied, "Even if your geology professor were here and said things I don't understand because I'm not a geologist, if what he says disagrees with the Bible, then he is wrong. If I can't explain why he is wrong, it only means I don't have the evidence to know the errors in his arguments. The Bible is the Word of God and is infallible. I'm sure I could get a creationist geologist to find out why your professor is wrong, because the Bible will always be right!"

Surely, as Christians blessed with the conviction that arises from the work of the Holy Spirit, we must accept the Bible as the infallible, authoritative Word of God—otherwise, we have nothing. If the Bible is to be questioned and cannot be trusted, and if it is continually subject to reinterpretation based on what men believe they have discovered, then we do not have an absolute authority. We do not have the Word of the One who knows everything, which means we have no basis for anything. Truth is spiritually discerned. Without the indwelling of the Holy Spirit there can be no real understanding.

PUBLIC SCHOOL AUDITORIUM
BAN RELIGION FROM SCHOOL
HUXLEY
ACLU
HUMANIST ASSOCIATION
OUR FIRST READING COMES FROM "ORIGIN OF THE SPECIES" PAGE 4....
EVOLUTION IS FACT
CARL SAGAN
ISAAC ASIMOV
DARWIN

CHAPTER 4

The Root of the Problem

Why do evolutionists not want to admit that evolution is really a religion?

It is related to the fact that whatever you believe about your origins does affect your whole world view, the meaning of life, etc. If there is no God and we are the result of chance random processes, it means there is no Absolute Authority. And if there is no one who sets the rules then everyone can do whatever he likes or hopes he can get away with. Evolution is a religion which enables people to justify writing their own rules. The sin of Adam was that he did not want to obey the rules God set, but do his own will. He rebelled against God, and we all suffer from this same sin: rebellion against the Absolute Authority. Evolution has become the so-called "scientific" justification for people to continue in this rebellion against God.

HUMANIST WORLD VIEW — RELATIVE MORALITY

CHRISTIAN WORLD VIEW — GOD SETS RULES

The Bible tells us in the book of Genesis that there is a true and reliable account of the origin and early history of life on earth. Increasing numbers of scientists are realizing that when you take the Bible as your basis and build your models of science and history upon it, all the evidence from the living animals and plants, the fossils and the cultures fits. This confirms that the Bible really is the Word of God and can be trusted totally.

The secular humanists, of course, oppose this because they cannot allow the possibility of God being Creator. They fight to have prayer, Bible readings and the teaching of creation forced out of the public school curriculum. They have deceived the public into thinking this is eliminating religion from schools and leaving a neutral situation. *This is simply not true!* **They haven't eliminated religion from the public school. They have eliminated Christianity and have replaced it with an anti-God religion—humanism.**

Most public schools have become institutions that train generations of school children in the religion of humanism. There is a minority of Christian teachers in the public school movement who do try to be the "salt of the earth" in such institutions. However, it is becoming increasingly difficult for them. There are also quite a number of Christian teachers who hide their light under a bushel—frightened of being consistent Christians in such a pagan environment. Some teachers have been threatened with termination of their employment if they are seen to be giving a Christian philosophy in the educational system.

We see extreme emotionalism in reaction to the creation ministries around the world because the evolutionist religion is being attacked by a totally different belief system. This emotionalism can be seen in the way in which the anticreationists talk about the issue. For instance, consider the quote from Dr. Michael Archer (Senior Lecturer in Zoology at the University of New South Wales) in *Australian Natural History*, Volume 21, Number 1: "Scientific Creationism is not just wrong; it is ludicrously implausible. It is a grotesque parody of human thought and a downright misuse of human intelligence. In short, to the Believer, it is an insult to God."

The real battle is aligned with the fact that these people do not want to accept Christianity because they will not accept that there is a God to whom they are answerable. Perhaps this is why one evolutionist lecturer said: "You will never convince me that evolution is religion." In other words, no matter what we were able to show him concerning the nature of evolution, he refused to accept that it was a religion. He did not want to accept that he had a faith because then he would have to admit it was a blind faith. And he would not be able to say that it was the right faith.

The public has genuinely been misled into thinking that evolution is **only** scientific and belief in God is **only** religious. Evolution is causing many people to stumble and not listen when Christians share with them the truth of the God of creation. You will notice in humanist opposition (through debates, the media, books, etc.) to the creation ministries that they very rarely identify any evidence for evolution. The main reason is, of course, that there is none.

Walk into a museum and have a look at all of the "evidence" for evolution on display. Different kinds of animals and plants are represented by carefully preserved specimens or by large numbers of fossils. You will see the story of evolution in words—but not in the evidence you see. The evidence is *in* the glass case. The hypothetical story of evolution can only be seen pasted on the glass case.

All the evolutionists have to do is to come up with one piece of evidence that proves evolution. If evolution is right and creation is nonsense, evolutionists have the media at their disposal to prove to everyone that evolution is true. However, they cannot do this. The evidence overwhelmingly supports exactly what the Bible says. It is a shame that creationists do not have the same media coverage to explain to the world the overwhelming evidence for the truth of creationism.

Let's face it, secular evolutionists must oppose creation ministries because, if what we are saying is right (and it is)—that God is Creator—then their whole philosophy is destroyed. The basis for their philosophy decrees there is no God. If evolution is not true, the only alternative is creation. That is why they will cling to the evolutionary philosophy even if the evidence is totally contradictory. It is really a spiritual question.

Some may say that if the evidence is so overwhelming that God created, surely people would believe this. In Romans 1:20 (NIV) we read, "For since the creation of the world God's invisible qualities—His eternal power and divine nature—have been clearly seen, being understood from what has been made, so that men are without excuse."

The Bible tells us that there is enough evidence in the world to convince people that God is Creator, and to condemn those who do not believe.

If that is so, and the evidence is all there, why don't people believe it? Is it because they do not want to believe it? The Apostle Peter states (II Peter 3:5, NIV) that in the last days men will deliberately forget that God created the world. This means there is a willfulness on their part not to believe.

The Bible also tells us that, "There is no one who understands, no one who seeks God" (Romans 3:11, NIV) and "For God, who said, Let light shine out of darkness, made His light shine in our hearts to give us the light of the knowledge of the glory of God in the face of Christ" (II Corinthians 4:6, NIV). In other words, it is God who opens our hearts to the truth. When we think of the story of the Pharaoh who would not let God's people leave Egypt, the Bible says, "But the Lord hardened Pharaoh's heart, and he was not willing to let them go" (Exodus 10:27). This idea is also recorded in Exodus 7:14 (NIV), " . . . Pharoah's heart is unyielding; he refuses to let the people go." In the New Testament we read that Jesus taught the Pharisees and scribes in parables saying: "In them is fulfilled the prophecy of Isaiah: You will be ever hearing but never understanding: you will be ever seeing but never perceiving. For this people's heart has become calloused; they hardly hear with their ears, and they have closed their eyes, otherwise they might see with their eyes, hear with their ears, understand with their hearts and turn, and I would heal them" (Matthew 13:14-15, NIV).

Romans 1:28 (NIV) tells us, "Furthermore, since they did not think it worthwhile to retain the knowledge of God, He gave them over to a depraved mind, to do what ought not to be done."

Thus, it is God who lets us see the truth—lets us see that the evidence is all there—that He is Creator. However, in a very real sense, there has to be a willingness on our part to want to see as well. Why can't the humanists, the evolutionists see that all the evidence supports exactly what the Bible says? It is because they do not want to see it. It is not because the evidence is not there. They refuse to allow the evidence to be correctly interpreted in the light of Biblical teaching.

In Isaiah 50:10 (NIV) we read, "Who among you fears the Lord and obeys the word of His servant? Let him who walks in the dark, who has no light, trust in the name of the Lord and rely on his God."

It is my prayer that those who oppose the Creator God will come to trust in Him as Lord and Savior. When we read the rest of Isaiah, chapter 50, it should make each of us pray more for humanists and evolutionists who want to walk in their own light—in the light of man. Isaiah 50:11 (NIV) states: "But now, all you who light fires and provide yourselves with flaming torches go, walk in the light of your fires and of the torches you have set ablaze. This is what you shall receive from my hand: You will lie down in torment."

We do not want this to be the fate of any human being. As the Lord says in His Word, it is not His desire that any should perish. However, God (who is a God of love) is also the God who is Judge, and He cannot look upon sin. Therefore, sin must be judged for what it is. However, God in His infinite mercy sent His only begotten Son, "For God so loved the world that he gave his one and only Son, that whoever believes in Him shall not perish but have eternal life" (John 3:16, NIV).

"In the beginning was the Word, and the Word was with God, and the Word was God. The same was in the beginning with God. All things were made by Him; and without him was not anything made that was made. In Him was life; and the life was the light of men" (John 1:1-4, KJV).

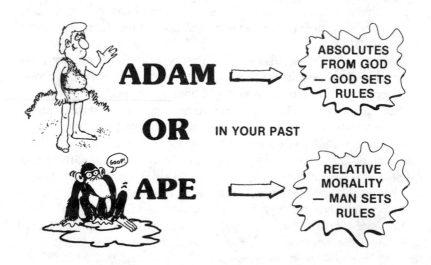

CHAPTER 5

Crumbling Foundations

Evolution has been popularized and presented as scientific truth, and many Christians have added evolutionary belief to their Biblical belief in God as Creator. Thus, while many Christians acknowledge that God created, they believe He used the process of evolution to bring all things into being. This is usually called "theistic evolution." Widespread confusion has resulted, causing many to question the plain statements of the Bible. Christians are no longer sure of what is truth and what is not. Too many Christians have not realized the foundational importance of the creation/evolution issue.

As already indicated, there is a connection between origins and issues affecting society such as marriage, clothing, abortion, sexual deviancy, parental authority, etc. How do we know what our beliefs should be in relation to these matters? Christians need to look deeply into the reasons why they believe as they do.

To begin to understand this, we must first consider the relevance of creation in Genesis. In John 5:46-47 (KJV) we read of Jesus' words, "For had ye believed Moses, ye would have believed Me: for he wrote of Me. But if ye believe not his writings, how shall ye believe My words?" Then in Luke 16:31 (KJV) Jesus quotes Abraham as saying, "If they hear not Moses and the prophets neither will they be persuaded, though one rose from the dead."

Both references underline the paramount importance placed on the writings of Moses, beginning with Genesis. In Luke 24:44 Jesus referred to the "Law of Moses" in an obvious reference to the five books of the Law (the Pentateuch), which includes Genesis, accepting Moses

as author. In Acts 28:23, we read that Paul, in Rome, preached unto them Jesus from Moses and the prophets. These are all references to the writings of Moses. And, there is one book of Moses that is referred to more often in the rest of the Bible than any other book. That book is Genesis. But in theological and Bible colleges, in Christian and non-Christian circles, which book of the Bible is the most attacked, mocked, scoffed at, thrown out, allegorized and mythologized? The book of *Genesis*! The very writings that are quoted from more than any other are the ones most attacked, disbelieved or ignored. Why is that so?

FOUNDATIONS UNDER ATTACK

Psalm 11:3 (NIV) asks, "When the foundations are being destroyed, what can the righteous do?"

It is important to understand the relationship that the psalmist is making. Society depends on moral foundations. By a mutual agreement which has sometimes been called a "social contract," man, in an ordered and civilized society, sets limits to his own conduct. However, when such obligations are repudiated and the law collapses along with the order it brings, what option has the man who seeks peace? The psalmist is looking at the fact that whenever the foundations of society are undermined, then what have good and righteous men done to prevent its impending collapse?

Some quite correctly quote the Scriptures in saying that Jesus Christ is the Foundation and He cannot be destroyed. In the context in which this verse from Psalm 11 is used, we are talking about the foundational knowledge upon which our moral framework is built. The foundational knowledge of Jesus Christ as Creator can be removed in people's thinking, whether they are from Australia, America, England or any other society. This action does not mean that Jesus Christ is not Creator, nor does it mean that He has been dethroned. However, it does mean that, in those nations that abandon this foundational basis, the whole fabric of society will suffer the consequences.

If you destroy the foundations of anything, the structure will collapse. If you want to destroy any building, you are guaranteed early success if you destroy the foundations.

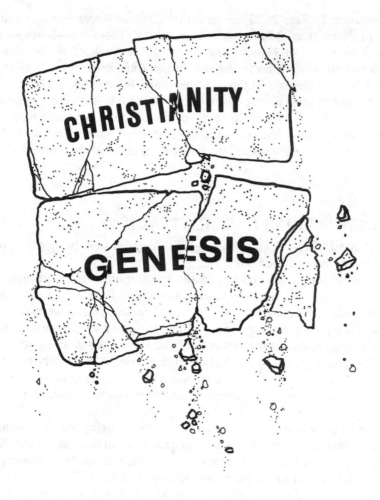

Likewise, if one wants to destroy Christianity, then destroy the foundations established in the book of Genesis. Is it any wonder that Satan is attacking Genesis more than any other book?

The Biblical doctrine of origins, as contained in the book of Genesis, is foundational to all other doctrines of Scripture. Refute or undermine in any way the Biblical doctrine of origins, and the rest of the Bible is compromised. **Every single Biblical doctrine of theology, directly or indirectly, ultimately has its basis in the book of Genesis.**

Therefore, if you do not have a believing understanding of that book, you cannot hope to attain full comprehension of what Christianity is all about. If we want to understand the meaning of anything, we must understand its origins—its basis.

Genesis is the only book that provides an account of the origin of all the basic entities of life and the universe: the origin of life, of man, of government, of marriage, of culture, of nations, of death, of the chosen people, of sin, of diet and clothes, of the solar system . . . the list is almost endless. The meaning of all these things is dependent on their origin. In the same way, the meaning and purpose of the Christian gospel depends on the origin of the problem for which the Savior's death was, and is, the solution.

How would you answer the following questions? Imagine someone coming up to you and saying, "Hey, Christian, do you believe in marriage? Do you believe it means one man for one woman for life? If so, why?" Now, the average Christian would say that he or she believes in marriage because it is somewhere in the Bible, Paul said something about it, that adultery is sin and there are some laws laid down about it.

If you are not a Christian, consider these questions: Are you married? Why? Why not just live with someone without bothering to marry? Do you believe marriage is one man for one woman for life? Why not six wives? Or six husbands? What happens if your son comes home and says, "Dad, I am going to marry Bill tomorrow." Would you say, "You can't do that, son! It's just not done!" What if your son replied, "Yes it is, Dad. There are even churches that will marry us." If you are not a Christian, what will you say to your son? Can you have any basis, any justification, for insisting that he should not have a homosexual lifestyle if he wants to?

When attempting to justify why they do or do not have a particular belief, many people today often have many *opinions* rather than *reasons*. It is sometimes interesting to watch interviews on television news programs. I recall one program on Australian television in which people were interviewed and asked to express their opinions concerning a government department's ruling to grant homosexual couples benefits similar to those received by married heterosexual couples. Many of the opinions expressed went like this: "It's not right." "It goes against my grain." "It's wrong." "It's not normal." "It's bad." "It shouldn't happen." "It's not good." "It shouldn't be allowed." "Why shouldn't they?" "People can do what they like!" And many other similar expressions were stated.

After I had spoken on creation at one public school, a student said to me, "I want to write my own rules about life and decide what I want to do."

I said, "You can do that if you like, son, but in that case, why can't I shoot you?"

He replied, "You can't do that!"

"Why not?"

"Because it's not right," he said.

I said to him, "Why is it not right?"

"Because it is wrong."

"Why is it wrong?"

He looked perplexed and said to me, "Because it is not right!"

This student had a problem. On what basis could he decide that something was right or wrong? He had started the conversation by indicating that he wanted to write his own rules. He was told that if he wanted to write his own rules, then surely I could write my rules. He certainly agreed with this. If that was so, and I could convince enough people to agree with me that characters like him were dangerous, then why should we not eliminate him from society? He then started to say to me again, "It's not right—it's wrong—it's not right." If he had no basis in an absolute authority that sets the rules, it was really a battle of his opinion versus my opinion. Perhaps the strongest or the cleverest would win. He got the point.

Many people have the opinion that a homosexual lifestyle is wrong. However, if it is just an opinion, then surely the view that homosexuality is acceptable is just as valid as any other view. The point is, it is not a matter of one's opinion. It is really a matter of what does the One who is the Creator, who owns us, give us as a basis for the principles governing this area of life? What does God say in His Word concerning this issue?

Christians have standards of right and wrong because they accept that there is a Creator and, as Creator, He has direct ownership over His creation. He owns us not only because He created us but because as the Scriptures say, " . . . You are not your own; you were bought at a price . . ." (I Corinthians 6:19-20, NIV). God created everything;

therefore, He has absolute authority. Because humans are created beings, they are under total obligation to the One who has absolute authority over them. Our Absolute Authority has a right to set the rules. It is in our own best interest to obey because He is Creator. Thus, what is right and what is wrong is not a matter of anyone's opinion, but must be in accord with the principles found in the Word of God, who has authority over us. Just as a car designer provides a manual for correct maintenance of what he has designed and made, so too does our Creator supply His creation with all the instructions that are necessary to live a full, free and abundant life. God has provided His set of instructions, not out of some spiteful or killjoy design, but because He loves us and knows what is best for us.

We often hear comments from parents that their children have rebelled against the Christian ethic, asking why they should obey their parents' rules. One major reason for this is that many Christian parents have not instructed their children from foundational perspectives concerning what they should or should not do. If children see rules as no more than parents' opinions, then why should they obey them? It does make an enormous difference when children are taught from the earliest age that God is Creator and that He has determined what is right and wrong. The rules come from God and, therefore, they must be obeyed. It is impossible to build any structure without a foundation, but that is what many parents are trying to do in the training of their children. The results of such attempts are all around us—a generation with increasing numbers rejecting God and the absolutes of Christianity.

At one church, a very sad father came to me and said, "My sons rebelled against Christianity. I remember their coming to me and saying, 'Why should we obey *your* rules?' I had never thought to tell them that they weren't my rules. I only realized this morning how I should have given them the foundations of God as Creator and explained that He sets the rules. I have the responsibility before Him as head of my house to see they are carried through. They only saw the Christian doctrines I was conveying to them as my opinions, or the church's opinions. Now they won't have anything to do with the church. They are doing what is right in their own eyes—not God's."

This is so typical of today's Christian society, and it is very much related to this issue of foundations. Many parents do not realize they are not laying the proper foundation at home by placing the emphasis on God as Creator. When their children go to school, they are given another foundation: God is not Creator and we are simply products of chance. No wonder so many children rebel. One cannot build a house from the roof down. We must start from the foundation and build upon this. Sadly, many parents have built a structure for the next generation which does not have the foundational understanding that Jesus Christ is the Creator.

Students in most of our schools are given a totally anti-Biblical foundation: the foundation of evolution. This foundation, of course, will not allow the Christian structure to stand. A structure of a different type—humanism—is the one built on this foreign foundation.

So many parents have said it was when their children went to high school or college that they drifted away from Christianity. Many rejected Christianity entirely. If there was never an emphasis on constructing the right foundation at home, it is little wonder the Christian structure collapsed. Regrettably, from my experience I have found that many Christian schools and colleges also teach evolution—so one should not assume that his children are necessarily safe because they are sent to a Christian school. The school may claim that it teaches creation, but, on a detailed investigation, it is often found that they teach that God used evolution in creation.

This same problem of a structure without a foundation is also reflected in another way. Many Christians may be against abortion, sexual deviancy and other moral problems in society, yet they cannot give proper justification for their opposition. Most Christians have an idea of what is wrong and what is right, but they do not understand why. This lack of reasons for our position is seen by others as just "opinions." And why should our opinion be any more valid than that of someone else?

All these issues relate to an understanding of what the Bible is all about. It is not just a guide-book for life. It is the very basis upon which all of our thinking must be built. Unless we understand that book, we will *not* have proper understanding of God and His relationship to man, and thus what a Christian world view is all about. That is why Jesus said in John 5:47 that we must believe the writings of Moses.

For instance, to understand why living as a homosexual is wrong,

one has to understand that the basis for marriage comes from Genesis. It is here we read that God ordained marriage and declared it to be one man for one woman for life. God created Adam and Eve, not Adam and Bruce! One primary importance for marriage as stated in Malachi 2:15, is that God created two to be "one" so that they could produce "a Godly seed" (i.e., Godly offspring). When one understands that there are specific roles which God ordained for men and women, one has reasons for standing against any legislation that weakens or destroys the family.

Thus, a homosexual lifestyle is anti-God, and so it is wrong, not because it is our opinion, but because God, the Absolute Authority,

says so. (Note particularly Leviticus 18:22, Romans 1:24, 26, 27, and Genesis 2:23, 24.)

We must reinforce in our own thinking, and in that of our Christian churches, that the Bible *is* the Word of God and that God has absolute authority over our lives. We must listen to what He says in relation to the principles to live by in **every area** of life, **regardless of what anyone's opinion is.** This human-based, opinion-orientated argument permeates the church in many ways. Consider the issue of abortion.

I have been to Bible studies where groups are discussing abortion. Many of the members give their opinion about what they think, but they give no reference to the Bible. They say such things as: "What if their daughter were raped," or "if the baby were going to be deformed," or "if somebody wouldn't be able to cope with looking after the child," then perhaps abortion would be acceptable. This is where our churches are falling by the wayside. The idea that everyone can have an opinion devoid of a basis in Biblical principles has crept into our churches and is one of the main reasons why we have so many problems sorting out doctrine and determining what we should believe. It is not a matter of autonomous human opinion about what is developing in a mother's womb—it is a matter of what God says in His Word concerning the principles that must govern our thinking. Psalm 139, Psalm 51, Jeremiah 1 and many other passages of Scripture make it quite plain that, at the point of conception, we are human beings. Therefore, abortion in all instances must be viewed as killing a human being. That is the only way of looking at the matter. It is time we woke up. When it comes to such issues, we must take God's view, not man's!

If we were less nervous about doing this, a lot of the problems we have in churches today would obviously be more easily solved. A large conference of one particular Protestant denomination was discussing whether or not the church should ordain women as pastors. It was interesting to see what happened. Someone jumped to his feet and said we should ordain women as pastors because they are just as bright as men. Another commented that we have women doctors and women lawyers, so why shouldn't we have women pastors? Somebody else said women are equal to men and, therefore, they should be pastors. But at this and other such conferences, how many people do we hear stating, "God made man; God made woman. He has given them their special roles in this world. The only way we could ever attempt to come to the right conclusion about this issue is to start from what He says concerning the roles of men and women." The trouble is, everyone wants to have his or her own opinion without reference to God's opinion.

At one meeting, a lady responded in a rather irate tone to what I had said about the roles of men and women. She said that she should not be submissive to her husband until he was as perfect as Christ. I then asked her where this was stated in the Bible. She said it was obvious that the Bible taught this. Therefore, she did not have to be in submission to her husband. I repeated my question to her, insisting she show me where in the Bible it made such a statement or gave a principle whereby one could come to that conclusion logically. She could not show me but still insisted that if her husband could not be as perfect as Christ she didn't have to be submissive to him. It was obvious to everyone present that she wanted her own opinion regardless of what the Scripture stated. She did not want to be submissive to her husband, and she did not want to obey the Scriptures.

Another place where we often hear people's opinions expressed in all sorts of ways is at members' meetings in churches. I have been to meetings where they were electing deacons. Someone would suggest a certain person to be a deacon because he was such a good man. When somebody else suggested that the qualifications for a deacon as given in the Scriptures should be applied, some objected, saying that you could not rule out a person from being a deacon just because he did not measure up to the qualifications given in Scripture. In other words, people's opinions according to some were above Scripture.

There are many ways in which we see this whole philosophy permeating our Christian society. The principal of a Christian school was telling me that he has a number of parents objecting to his strict discipline, which is based upon Biblical principles. Their objections usually took the form of comparison with other schools, or saying that their children were not as bad as other children around the neighborhood. Instead of comparing the standards with God's Word, they compared them with other people. For instance, some parents insisted that because there were other students in the school who had not been caught doing wrong things, their children should not be punished. The principal pointed out that if this was applied in society there would be enormous problems. For example, does this mean that police should not prosecute a driver they happen to catch with a high alcohol content in his blood just because many other drivers who also have a high alcohol content were not caught? These parents were upset because of the standard the principal applied—a standard based upon the authority of God's Word.

Paul says, "Stand fast, and hold the traditions which ye have been taught . . ." (II Thessalonians 2:15, KJV). Do we stand fast, or do we waver? What we are seeing in our society is an outward expression, in more and more of its naked ferocity, of the rejection of God and His absolutes, and the growing belief that only human opinions matter.

The reason for much of the conflict throughout the church at the present time is that people are fighting over their opinions. It is not a matter of opinion, yours or mine. It is what *God* says that matters. The basis for our thinking should be the principles from His Word. They must determine our actions. To understand this, we must also appreciate that Genesis is foundational to the entire Christian philosophy. One major difficulty in our churches is that many people do not trust Genesis. Consequently, they do not know what else in the Bible to trust. They treat the Bible as an interesting book containing some vague sort of religious truth. This view is destroying the church and our society, and it is time religious leaders wake up to the fact. Not to take Genesis 1 through 11 literally is to do violence to the rest of Scripture.

As Professor James Barr, a renowned Hebrew scholar and Oriel Professor of the Interpretation of Holy Scripture at Oxford University, said in a personal letter on April 23, 1984, "So far as I know there is no Professor of Hebrew or Old Testament at any world-class university who does not believe that the writer(s) of Genesis 1 through 11 intended to convey to their readers the ideas that (a) creation took place in a series of six days which were the same as the days of 24 hours we now experience; (b) the figures contained in the Genesis genealogies provided by simple addition a chronology from the beginning of the world up to later stages in the Biblical story; (c) Noah's flood was understood to be world-wide and extinguished all human and animal life except for those in the ark."

Please note that many, if not most of these "world-class" scholars do not believe in the Bible or Christianity anyway, so they are not interested in "wresting" the Scriptures to somehow try to make their religion fit with evolution. They are just expressing their opinion on the plain meaning of the text. Disbelieve it if you wish, but it is impossible to make out that it is saying anything other than what it does say. We can see now that those who say that the clear teaching of Genesis is not what it actually means are not doing so on the basis of literary or linguistic scholarship, but because of partial surrender to the pressure of evolutionary thinking.

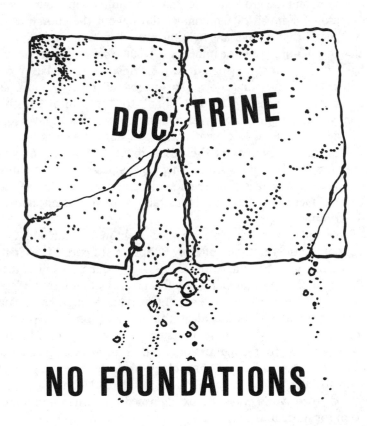

CHAPTER 6

Genesis Does Matter

Let us look in detail at some important Christian doctrines, to show why this emphasis on a literal Genesis must be accepted.

Suppose that we are being questioned concerning the doctrines Christians believe. Think carefully how you would answer in detail.

Why do we believe in marriage?

Why do we promote the wearing of clothes?

Why are there rules—right and wrong?

Why are we sinners—what does that mean?

Why is there death and suffering in the world?

Why is there to be a new heaven and a new earth?

We will consider each one carefully, as it is important to have reasons for what we believe. In fact, God expects His children to be ready to give answers—to give reasons for what they believe. In I Peter 3:15 (KJV) we read, "But sanctify the Lord God in your hearts: and be ready always to give an answer to every man that asketh you a reason of the hope that is in you with meekness and fear."

Christianity, as distinct from atheism, is not a "blind" faith, but an objective one . . . our object is Jesus Christ. He does reveal Himself to those who come by faith believing that He is. John 14:21 (KJV) says, "and I will love him, and will manifest myself to him." Hebrews 11:6b (KJV): "for he that cometh to God must believe that He is, and that He is a rewarder of them that diligently seek Him."

If reasons for the validity of the Christian's faith are not forthcoming, his witness is weakened and open to ridicule. Christians must be prepared to make an intelligent defense of the Gospel by arming themselves with knowledge and an understanding of the forms unbelief takes in these days. Many Christians do not know how to communicate the fact that God's Word and God's laws are true. The net result is generations of wishy-washy Christians who believe in many things, but are not sure why. Personal witnessing can lose its impact if the Christian fails to share intelligent reasons for his faith. This must be avoided, lest ridicule and dishonor come to the name of Christ.

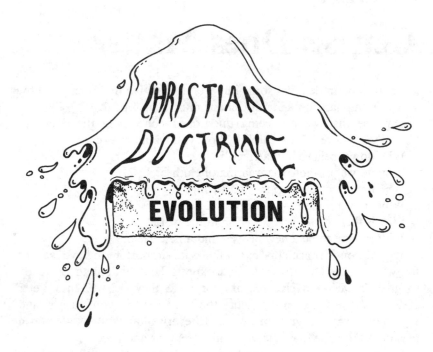

A good example of what happens when we do not give reasons for what we believe can be seen in a letter to the editor in an Arizona newspaper. It reads as follows: "When I was a youngster, we all believed that men had one less rib than women because God created Eve with one of Adam's ribs. When the story was written five to ten thousand years later after Noah and the world flood, how many people could read, much less write? . . . You say you are a teacher of creationism in school classes. How would you answer these questions? If Noah took two of each animal on the ark, where did he get polar bears, bison and kangaroos? You might answer that those animals lived in the Eastern Mediterranean area back then. The next question would be, how did the various colors of humans evolve from one white (deeply tanned) family in 5,000 or even 50,000 years? . . . When I was growing up in a deeply religious family, I was told not to question the Bible and other religious writings. I got no answers then, and 70 years later I am still waiting for a reasonable explanation."

I personally spoke to the writer of this letter. As we talked, it became obvious that he had been told to accept the Bible by blind faith and was never given any useful answers. Omission caused him to reject evangelical Christianity. How sad! And the answers to these sorts of questions are available today. So, let us "give reasons for what we believe" as we discuss the subjects mentioned above.

FOUNDATIONAL KNOWLEDGE

MARRIAGE

When Jesus was asked concerning divorce in Matthew 19 (KJV), He immediately referred to the origin, and thus the foundation, of marriage. He said, "Have ye not read, that He which made them at the beginning made them male and female? And said, For this cause shall a man leave his father and mother, and shall cleave unto his wife: and they twain shall be one flesh?" And from where did Jesus quote? Genesis! (In fact, He quoted from Genesis, chapters 1 and 2, in the same verse—those who wrongly say Genesis 1 and 2 are two different accounts of creation should refer to Appendix 1.) Jesus was saying: "Don't you understand there is a historical basis for marriage?" If we did not have this historical basis, we would not have marriage. The only basis is in the Scriptures. You can say it is convenient for you, but you cannot tell your son he cannot marry Bill or, for that matter, marry Julie and Susan. Likewise, extramarital relationships would be a tolerable alternative. You would have no justification for thinking otherwise.

Now, if we go back to Genesis, we read how God took dust and made a man. From the man's side, He made a woman. Adam's first recorded words were: "This is now bone of my bones and flesh of my flesh." They were one flesh. When a man and a woman marry, they become one. This is the historical basis. Also, we are to cleave to one another as if we had no parents—just like Adam and Eve who had no parents. We know it is to be a heterosexual relationship. Why? Because, as stated before, God made Adam and Eve (a man and a woman—*not* a man and a man). That is the only basis for marriage, and that is why we know that homosexual behavior and desire is an evil, perverse, and unnatural deviation. It is time the church stood its ground against the increasing acceptance of homosexuality as something natural or normal or as an "acceptable alternative." Paul would not have written about homosexuality in the way that he did in Romans if he did not have that historical basis. (Please note that although as Christians we condemn the sin of homosexuality, we are to be grace oriented toward the homosexual and seek his or her deliverance from bondage.)

What about the rest of the teaching on marriage? There is another aspect which has to do with the family. It is the reason many Christian families go to pieces or the offspring go astray. In the majority of Christian homes today, it is usually the mother who teaches the children spiritually. What an unfortunate thing it is that fathers have not embraced their God-given responsibility. When one looks at the Biblical roles given to fathers and mothers, it is the fathers who are allocated the responsibility of providing for their children, and providing the family's spiritual and physical needs (Isaiah 38:19, Proverbs 1:8, Ephesians 6:4). One result of this role reversal is that the sons often stop coming to church. Christian girls who have not been trained properly by their fathers concerning the marriage relationship often disobey the Lord by dating and marrying non-Christian men.

A young woman approached me and said that she was married to a non-Christian. She explained that, when she was dating this man, she compared him to her father and saw no real difference. Yet, her father was a Christian. Because her father was not the spiritual head of the house, she did not see any real difference between him and the person she was dating. She saw no reason to make sure that her husband-to-be was a Christian. Now that she is married and has children, there are some extreme problems with their marriage regarding the bringing up of their children.

A major reason for so many problems in Christian families today is that fathers have not taken their God-commanded responsibility of being priest in their household. As a husband and a father, he is also a priest to his wife and children. It is not, however, a "boss" relationship where men despotically lord it over women. Female liberationists think the Bible teaches a tyrannical relationship in marriage. Unfortunately, many Christians think like this also. However, the Bible does not say this at all. Anyone who uses these Biblical role absolutes to justify one person's seeking power over another has completely missed the whole message of Jesus Christ (Ephesians 5:22-33, John 13:5). The Bible also says we are to submit one to another (Ephesians 5:21). If you do not adopt the God-given roles set out in Scripture, you will find that your family will not function as intended, and problems usually follow. The Bible also tells husbands to love their wives as Christ loved the church (Ephesians 5:25). In many instances, if husbands loved their wives this way it would make it easier for many women to be submissive to them.

WHY CLOTHES?

Consider why we wear clothes. Is it to keep warm? What then if we lived in the tropics? Is it to look nice? If these are our only reasons, why wear clothes? Why not take them off when we want to, where we want to? Does it really matter if one goes nude publicly? Ultimately, the only reason for insisting that clothes must be worn is a moral one. If there is a moral reason, it must have a basis somewhere; therefore, there must be standards connected to the moral reason. What then are the standards? Many in our culture (including Christians) just accept the fashions of the day. Parents, what about the training of your children? What do you say to them about clothes?

FOUNDATIONAL KNOWLEDGE

CLOTHING

GENESIS

In her paper on "Greek Clothing Regulations: Sacred and Profane" (*Zeitschrift fur Papyrologie und Epigraphie, Band 55-1984*), Harrianne Mills has this to say: "Since the demise, roughly one hundred years ago, of the Biblically based theory that clothes are worn because of modesty, various theories have been put forward by anthropologists concerned with the origins and functions of clothing."

Why do we wear clothes? There is a moral basis if you go back to the Scriptures. We read in Genesis that when God made Adam and Eve they were naked. But sin came into the world, and sin distorts everything. Sin distorts nakedness. Immediately Adam and Eve knew they were naked, and they tried to make coverings out of fig leaves.

God came to their rescue, providing garments by killing an innocent animal. This was the first blood sacrifice; it was a covering for their sin.

Men are very easily aroused sexually. That is why seminaked women are used in television and magazine advertisements. Parents need to explain to their daughters how easily a man is aroused sexually by a woman's body. They need to know, because many of them do not understand what happens to a man. At one church, after I had spoken on the topic of clothing, a young woman came up and told me that she had only been a Christian for six months. She was dating a young Christian man and was perplexed as to why he often told her not to wear certain things. Every time she asked him why, he started to feel embarrassed. She had not realized before that what she wore (or did not wear) could put a stumbling block in a man's way by causing him to commit adultery in his heart.

Fathers need to explain to their daughters about how men react to a woman's body. They also need to explain to their sons that although women's clothes, or lack of them, can be a stumbling block to a male, it is not an excuse for them in relation to what their mind does with what they see. Job had an answer for this problem: "I made a covenant with my eyes not to look lustfully at a girl" (Job 31:1, NIV). As Christians, males should have a covenant with their eyes and be reminded of this when lustful thoughts come as a result of what they see or hear.

Jesus states that, if a man lusts after a woman in his heart, he commits adultery in his heart: "But I tell you that anyone who looks at a woman lustfully has already committed adultery with her in his heart" (Matthew 5:28, NIV). Sin distorts nakedness. Even the perfect relationship experienced by Adam and Eve before the Fall degenerated. After the Fall, they hid from God and were ashamed of their nakedness. Many Christian women wear clothes that really accentuate their sexuality. And many a roving eye follows every movement. But what is happening? Men are committing adultery in their hearts. Adultery for which they and the women will have to answer.

In many Christian homes the parents have certain beliefs about clothing. They say to their teenagers, "You can't wear that." The teenagers reply, "But why not?" "Because it is not the Christian thing," answer the parents. "Why not?" ask the teenagers again. "Because

Christians don't wear that," the parents insist. "Why not?" the reply comes.

Then you often hear daughters saying, "You're old-fashioned, Mom and Dad." They are saying that their parents have one opinion but they have another opinion. For the most part, children are going to stick with their own opinion. However, it is not a matter of the parents' opinion or the child's opinion. In order for the parents to "save face," they often resort to an imposed legalism. What a difference it makes when the parents use Genesis as a basis to explain to their children why they must do this or that with regard to clothing, particularly if they have already solidly trained their children that God is Creator, He sets the rules, and Genesis is foundational to all doctrine. It is infinitely better than parents saying, "This is what you *will* do," and imposing this standard on their children with no basis. However, as we read in Ephesians 6:1 (KJV), "Children, obey your parents in the Lord: for this is right." Children must obey their parents, and that is not a matter of their opinion, either.

There is a moral basis for wearing clothes because of what sin has done to nakedness. We must understand how men are created. Man was designed to be easily aroused sexually and to respond to one woman (his wife). This was, and is, necessary for procreation in marriage. However, sin distorts this, and it is wrong for a man to look lustfully on any woman other than his wife. Therefore, clothing should minimize to the greatest extent any stumbling block laid in a man's way. But a man is no less guilty if he succumbs to the "second look." One should not simply accept the fashions of the day. There is a moral basis for clothing; therefore, there are standards. Knowing what men are like and knowing what sin does to nakedness, we thus have a basis for understanding what the standards should be.

WHY LAW AND MORALITY?

What do you tell your children about laws? Perhaps you tell them some things are right and some are wrong, but do you ever explain to them the origin of right and wrong? Would you say we have right and wrong because God has given us laws? If so, why is that? Why does He have a right to say what is right and what is wrong?

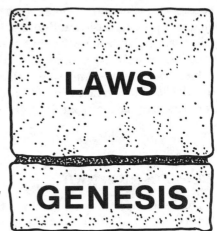

Why is there right and wrong (e.g., the Ten Commandments)? Remember the story in Matthew 19:16-17 (KJV) when the man came to Jesus and said to Him: "Good Master, what good thing shall I do, that I may have eternal life?" Jesus replied, "Why callest thou Me good? There is none good but one, that is, God . . . " How do you decide if something is right or wrong or good or bad? God, the only One who is good, created us and, therefore, owns us. Thus, we are obligated to Him, and we must obey Him. He has the right to set the rules. He knows everything there is to know about everything (i.e., has absolute knowledge), and therefore we must obey. That is why we have absolutes, why there are standards, and why there is right and wrong.

Now, if you are *not* a Christian and you think some things are right and some are wrong, why do you think like that? You have no basis for such a decision. How do you arrive at your standards? How do you decide what is good and bad? Most non-Christians who believe there is right and wrong are practicing the Christian ethic.

Atheistic evolutionary philosophy says: "There is no God. All is the result of chance and randomness. Death and struggle are the order of the day, not only now, but indefinitely into the past and future."

If this is true, there is no basis for right and wrong. The more people believe in evolution, the more they are going to say, "There is no God. Why should I obey authority? Why should there be rules against aberrant sexual behavior? Why should there be rules concerning abortion? After all, evolution tells us we are all animals. So, killing babies by abortion is no worse than chopping the head off a fish or a chicken." It *does* matter whether you believe in evolution or creation! It affects every area of your life.

"FOR BY THE LAW IS THE KNOWLEDGE OF SIN" (ROMANS 3:20b, NKJ)

This issue comes down to the simple fact explained by Paul in Romans 3:20 (KJV), "For by the law is the knowledge of sin." In Romans 7:7 he continues: "I had not known sin, but by the law."

The existence of God is nowhere defended by Scripture. This fact is taken as being obvious. Who He is and what He has done is clearly explained. Neither is there any doubt as to His sovereign authority over His creation or what our attitude should be toward Him as Creator. He has the right to set the rules. We have the responsibility to obey and rejoice in His goodness, or disobey and suffer His judgment.

Adam, the first man, made this choice. He chose to rebel. Sin is rebellion against God and His will. Genesis tells us that this first act of human rebellion took place in the Garden of Eden.

To understand what sin is all about—that all mankind are sinners— and how to recognize sin, God gave us the Law. He had the right and the loving concern to do this. He is Creator, and His character allows for no less. All-powerful, all-loving, all-gracious, He has laid down for us the rules by which we must live if our lives are to develop in the way they should. As Paul says in Romans 7:7, "For I had not known lust, except the law had said thou shalt not covet."

The Bible clearly teaches that each human being is a sinner, in a state of rebellion against God. Initially, the Law was given, as Paul states, to explain sin. But, knowing about sin was not a solution to the problem of sin. More was needed. The Creator had not forgotten His commitment to and love of His creation, for He set the payment and paid the price—*Himself.* God's Son, the Lord Jesus Christ, who is God, suffered the curse of death on a cross and became sin for us so that God could pour out His judgment upon sin. But, just as all die in Adam, so all who believe in Christ's atoning death and resurrection live in Him.

Those who oppose the Creator are opposing the One who is the Absolute Authority—the One who sets the rules and *keeps them.*

In the book of Judges it is stated: "In those days there was no king in Israel; but every man did that which was right in his own eyes" (Judges 17:6, KJV). People today are little different. They want evolution taught as fact and the belief in creation banished because they, too, want to be a law unto themselves. They want to maintain the rebellious nature they have inherited from Adam, and they will *not* accept the authority of the One who, as Creator and Law-Giver, has the right to tell them exactly what to do. This really is what the creation/evolution conflict is all about. Does God the Creator have the right to tell a person what he must do with his life? Or, can man decide for himself what he wants to do without suffering the consequences? These are not rhetorical questions. Their very nature demands an answer from every individual. Thus, it comes down to whether or not man is autonomous, and therefore can decide everything for himself, or whether he is owned by God. Most want to be autonomous and believe they can act according to their own desires and understanding. But, man is not autonomous, and there the battle rages.

The Bible tells us that those who trust in the Lord, and are indwelt by His Holy Spirit, will show the fruit of the Spirit: "love, joy, peace, long-suffering, gentleness, goodness, faith, meekness, temperance" (Galatians 5:22-23, KJV). Those who are not indwelt by the Spirit of God, and who reject the God of Creation, will reflect the fruit of this rejection: "adultery, fornication, uncleanness, lasciviousness, idolatry, witchcraft, hatred, variance, emulations, wrath, strife, seditions, heresies, envyings, murders, drunkenness, revellings and such like" (Galatians 5:19-21, KJV). The Bible states clearly that corrupt roots bring forth evil fruit. Pornography, abortion, homosexuality, lawlessness, euthanasia, infanticide, loose morals, unfaithfulness in marriage and other such things—practices which are becoming more and more prevalent in today's society—are certainly fruit of corrupt roots. They are the corrupt roots of evolution firmly entrenched in the compost of humanistic thinking.

Evolution is an anti-God religion held by many people today as justification for their continued pursuit of self-gratification and their rejection of God as Creator.

Many today will not accept that they are sinners. They do not want to accept that they must bow their knees before the God of Creation. They do not want to accept that anyone has authority over them with the right to tell them what to do.

Even many in our churches do not understand what is meant when man is described as "sinful." Many preachers (even many who consider themselves evangelical) think that the definition of sin can be limited to such things as adultery, alcoholism, heroin addiction, nudity, x-rated movies and bad language. However, sin does not stop here. We must understand that sin affects every area of our lives. Sin has an influence on every aspect of our culture. We must understand that sin pervades the whole of our thinking, and will, therefore, affect the whole of our actions. Jesus said, "For out of the heart come evil thoughts, murder, adultery, sexual immorality, theft, false testimony, slander" (Matthew 15:19, NIV).

We must understand that God is the Creator and Law-Giver, and every human must kneel in submission to Him. That there will come a time when all will do this is clearly recorded by Paul in Philippians 2:10-11 (KJV): "That at the name of Jesus every knee should bow, of things in heaven, and things on earth, and things under the earth, and every tongue should confess that Jesus Christ is Lord, to the glory of God the Father."

God's Word (the infallible Word of the perfect Creator) has to be the basis of our thinking. God, the Creator, is the One who provides the blueprint for happy and stable human relationships. If His Word is heeded, He supplies the basis for a true Christian philosophy for every area of human existence—agriculture, economics, medicine, politics, law enforcement, arts, music, sciences, family relationships—*every aspect of life*. In other words, there is a whole Christian way of thinking. There are foundational Biblical principles that govern every area of life. The Creator has not left His creatures without an instruction manual.

"THY WORD IS TRUE FROM THE BEGINNING" (PSALM 119:160, KJV).

Man's rejection of God as Creator (not starting with His Word as a basis for thinking in every area and not being submissive to Him) has resulted in the problems we have in society. This was painfully highlighted in a Letter to the Editor of an Australian newspaper. Apparently, a country newspaper was approached for placement of an advertisement requesting a married couple for farm work. They were told there would be no printing of an advertisement that contained the words, "married couple." The problem was apparently one of "discrimination." The term "married couple" had to be replaced with "two persons." It didn't matter which two persons applied for the job! The question: "On whose authority can't this be printed?" The answer: "The Human Rights Commission." The writer of the letter was justifiably horrified. However, this incident is the fruit of evolutionist thinking, and we can only expect similar instances to increase.

"OH LORD—OPEN OUR EYES THAT WE MAY SEE" (PSALM 119:18).

Concerned and convinced Christians must pray that the Lord will make clear to everyone the frightening direction in which man's rebellion is heading. Christians need to establish firmly the fact that God is Creator and that He has given us His law. We need to recognize what sin is and what the results of sinful existence are. We need to proclaim deliverance from sin through faith in Jesus Christ. Apart from this, there will be no rectifying the situation. **An all-out attack on evolutionist thinking is possibly the only real hope our nations have of rescuing themselves from an inevitable social and moral catastrophe.**

It is not easy for any human being to acknowledge that if there is a Creator we must be in submission to Him. However, there is no alternative. Man must recognize that he is in rebellion against the One who created him. Only then will man understand the Law, understand what sin is and understand the steps necessary to bring about the changes in individual lives that can ultimately effect changes in society.

The more our society rejects the creation basis and God's laws, the more it will degenerate spiritually and morally. This has happened many times throughout history and should stand as a warning. Let us consider a modern-day example.

THE CONSEQUENCES OF REJECTING GOD AND HIS ABSOLUTES.

Missionaries were sent to New Guinea because there were many so-called pagan and primitive people there. The story is told of one cannibal tribe, which has since ceased to be cannibalistic. Previously, men would race into a village, grab a man by the hair, pull him back, tense his abdominal muscles, use a bamboo knife to slit upon his abdomen, pull out his intestines, cut up his fingers, and while he was still alive, eat him until he died. People hear that and say, "Oh, what primitive savages!" They are not "primitive" savages; their ancestor was a man called Noah. The Indians' ancestor was a man called Noah; the Eskimos' ancestor was a man called Noah; and our ancestor was a man called Noah. Noah had the knowledge of God and could build ships. His ancestors could make musical instruments and they practiced agriculture. What happened to those New Guinea natives is that, somewhere in history (as Romans 1 tells us), they rejected the knowledge of God and His laws. And God turned them over to foolish, perverse and degenerate things.[1]

However, this same degeneracy (this same rejection of God's laws) can be seen in so-called civilized nations that cut people up alive all year long (one and a half million of them in the United States each year), and it is legalized. This is what abortion is—cutting up people alive and sucking out the bits and pieces. The so-called "primitive tribes" had ancestors who once knew the true God and His laws. As they rejected the true God of creation, their culture degenerated in every

---

[1]Although most anthropologists would deny there were or are cannibals in New Guinea, this story and others were related by missionaries who had spent most of their lives in that country. There are a number of books published documenting stories of cannibalism in New Guinea, e.g., *Headhunter*, Anzea Publishers, 1982.

area. The more our so-called "civilized nations" reject the God of creation, the more they will degenerate to a "primitive culture." Thus, a culture should not be interpreted according to whether they are primitive or advanced (as presupposed by the evolutionary scale), but every aspect of their culture must be judged against the standards of God's Word. How does your nation measure up?

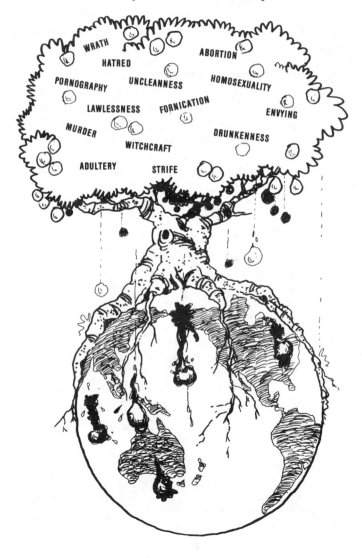

CHAPTER 7

Death—A Curse and a Blessing

WHY SIN AND DEATH?

Suppose someone came up to you and said, "You Christians are saying that we need Jesus Christ, and that we need to confess our sins. Sin? Why do we need Christ anyway? Besides, God can't be who He says He is. If He is, like you say, a God of love, look at all the death and suffering in the world. How can that be?" What would you say?

THE GOSPEL, SIN AND DEATH

What is the Gospel message? When God made man, He made him perfect. He made the first two people, Adam and Eve, and placed them in the Garden of Eden where they had a special, very beautiful relationship with God. When He made them, He gave them a choice. He wanted their love, not as a programmed response, but as a reasoned act. They chose to rebel against God. This rebellion is called sin. All sin comes under the banner of rebellion against God and His will.

As a result of that rebellion in Eden, a number of things happened. First, man was estranged from God. That separation is called spiritual death. On its own, the final effect of this would have been living for ever in our sinful bodies, eternally separated from God. Imagine living with Hitler and Stalin for ever! Imagine living in an incorrigible, sinful state for eternity. But something else happened. Romans 5:12 tells us that as a result of man's actions came sin, and as a result of sin came death; but not just spiritual death, as some theologians claim. To confirm this, one needs only read I Corinthians 15:20 (NIV) where Paul talks about the physical death of the **first Adam** and the physical death of Christ, the **last Adam.** Or read Genesis 3, where God expelled Adam and Eve from the Garden so that they would not eat of the Tree of Life and live forever. Physical death as well as spiritual death resulted from their sin.

Why did God send death? Three aspects of death should be considered carefully:

1. God, as a righteous judge, cannot look upon sin. Because of His very nature and the warning He gave to Adam, God had to judge sin. He had warned Adam that, if he ate of the tree of the knowledge of good and evil " . . . in the day that thou eatest thereof thou shalt surely die." The curse of death placed upon the world was, and is, a just and righteous judgment from God who is the Judge.

2. One of the aspects of man's rebellion was separation from God. The loss of a loved one through death shows the sadness of the separation between those left behind and the one who has departed this world. When we consider how sad it is when a loved one dies, it should remind us of the terrible consequences of sin that separated Adam from the perfect relationship he had with God. This separation involved all mankind, because Adam sinned as the representative of all.

3. Another aspect of death which many people miss is that God sent death because He loved us so much. God is love, and, strange as it may sound, we should really praise Him for that curse He placed on us. It was not God's will that man be cut off from Him for eternity. Imagine living in a sinful state for eternity, separated from God. But He loved us too much for that, and He did a very wonderful thing. In placing on us the curse of physical death, He provided a way to redeem man back to Himself. In the person of Jesus Christ, He suffered that curse on the cross for us. "He tasted death for every man" (Hebrews 2:9, KJV). By Himself becoming the perfect sacrifice for our sin of rebellion, He conquered death. He took the penalty which should rightly have been ours at the hands of a righteous Judge, and bore it in

His own body on the cross.

All who believe in Jesus Christ as Lord and Savior are received back to God to spend eternity with Him. Isn't that a wonderful message? *That is the message of Christianity.* Man forfeited his special position through sin, and as a result God placed upon him the curse of death so he could be redeemed back to God. What a wonderful thing God did! Every time we celebrate the Lord's Supper, we remember Christ's death and the awfulness of sin. Each Lord's day we rejoice in Christ's resurrection and thus the conquering of sin and death.

But evolution destroys the very basis of this message of love. The evolutionary process is supposed to be one of death and struggle, cruelty, brutality and ruthlessness. It is a ghastly fighting for survival, elimination of the weak and deformed. This is what underlies evolution—death, bloodshed and struggle bringing man into existence. Death over millions of years. It is an onward, upward "progression" leading to man. Yet, what does the Bible say in Romans 5:12? Man's actions led to sin, which led to death. The Bible tells us that without the shedding of blood there can be no remission of sins (Hebrews 9:22). God instituted death and bloodshed so that man could be redeemed. If death and bloodshed existed before Adam sinned, the basis for atonement is destroyed. (For a detailed discussion on this issue, see the book, *Man: Ape or Image*, listed in the resource section at the end of this book.)

Evolutionists would say death and struggle led to man's existence. The Bible says man's rebellious actions led to death. These statements cannot both be true. One denies the other—they are diametrically opposed. That is why the compromisers who claim to hold both positions at the same time (theistic evolutionists) are destroying the basis of the Gospel. If life formed in an onward "progression," how did man fall upward? What is sin? Sin would then be an inherited animal characteristic, not something due to the fall of man through disobedience. The many Christians who accept the belief of evolution and add God to it destroy the very foundation of the Gospel message they profess to believe.

At one church, a man came up to me and insisted that a Christian could believe in evolution. Since I had spent considerable time during the service showing that the Bible teaches there was no death before the Fall, I asked him whether he believed there was death before Adam fell? In an angry tone he asked me, "Do you beat your wife?" This took me aback a little, and I was not really sure of the point he was trying to make, so I asked him what he meant by that. He asked me again, "Do you beat your wife?" Then he walked off. Life is full of interesting experiences on the preaching trail. However, I thought about this man's comments for quite some time and then realized, after talking to a psychologist, that there is a type of question you can ask and no matter whether you answer no or yes you are trapped. Actually, what this man should have asked me was, "Have you stopped beating your wife?" If you answer either yes or no, you are admitting that you beat your wife. In relation to the death issue and Adam's Fall, if the man had answered in the affirmative, "Yes, there was death before Adam's fall," he would be admitting to a belief in something that contradicted the Bible. If he answered no, then he was denying evolution. Either way, he was showing that one cannot add evolution to the Bible. He was trapped, and he knew it.

I need to state here emphatically that I am not saying that if you believe in evolution you are not a Christian. There are many Christians who, for varying reasons (whether it be out of ignorance of what evolution teaches, pride, or a liberal view of the Scriptures) believe in evolution. Those who do believe in evolution are being inconsistent and, in reality, are destroying the foundations of the Gospel message. Therefore, I would plead with them to seriously consider the evidence against the position they hold.

Even atheists realize the inconsistency in Christians' believing in evolution, as seen in a quotation from an article by G. Richard Bozarth entitled, "The Meaning of Evolution," from *The American Atheist*, September 1978, page 19: "Christianity is—must be—totally committed to the special creation as described in Genesis, and Christianity must fight with all its full might, fair or foul, against the theory of evolution . . . . It becomes clear now that the whole justification of Jesus' life and death is predicated on the existence of Adam and the forbidden fruit he and Eve ate. Without the original sin, who needs to be redeemed? Without Adam's fall into a life of constant sin terminated by death, what purpose is there to Christianity? None."

The atheist Jacques Monod (noted for his contributions to molecular biology and philosophy) said in an interview titled "The Secret of Life," broadcast by the Australian Broadcasting commission on June 10, 1976, as a tribute to him: "Selection is the blindest, and most cruel way

of evolving new species, and more and more complex and refined organisms . . . the more cruel because it is a process of elimination, of destruction. The struggle for life and the elimination of the weakest is a horrible process, against which our whole modern ethic revolts. An ideal society is a non-selective society, it is one where the weak are protected; which is exactly the reverse of the so-called natural law. *I am surprised that a Christian would defend the idea that this is the process which God more or less set up in order to have evolution"* (emphasis mine).

Original sin, with death as a result, is the basis of the Gospel. That is why Jesus Christ came and what the Gospel is all about. If the first Adam is only an allegorical figure, then why not the last Adam (I Corinthians 15:45-47), Jesus Christ? If man did not really fall into sin, there is no need for a Savior. Evolution destroys the very foundations of Christianity because it states, "death is, and always has been, part of life." Now, if you lived in a skyscraper, and if there were people underneath that skyscraper with jackhammers hammering away at the foundations, would you say, "So what?" That is what many Christians are doing. They are being bombarded with evolution through the media, the public school system, television, newspapers, and yet they rarely react. The foundations of the "skyscraper" of Christianity are being eroded by the "jackhammers" of evolution. But, inside the skyscraper, what are many Christians doing? They are either sitting there doing nothing or are throwing out jackhammers saying, "Here, have a few more! Go destroy our foundations!"

Worse still, theistic evolutionists (those who believe in both evolution and God) are actively helping to undermine the basis of the Gospel. As the psalmist asks in Psalm 11:3 (NIV), "When the foundations are being destroyed what can the righteous do?" If the basis of the Gospel is destroyed, the structure built on that foundation (the Christian church) will largely collapse. If Christians wish to preserve the structure of Christianity, they must protect its foundation and therefore actively oppose evolution.

NEW HEAVENS AND NEW EARTH

Paradise Restored

Evolution also destroys the teaching of the new heavens and the new earth. What are we told about the new heavens and the new earth? Acts 3:21 says there will be a restoration (restitution). That means things will be restored to at least what they were originally. We read about what it will be like: "They shall not hurt nor destroy in all my holy mountain" (Isaiah 11:9, KJV). There will be vegetarianism and no violence. "The wolf also shall dwell with the lamb, and the leopard shall lie down with the kid; and the calf and the young lion and the fatling together; and a little child shall lead them . . . and the lion shall eat straw like an ox" (Isaiah 11:6-7, KJV)—that is vegetarian! "And there shall be no more curse" (Revelation 22:3, KJV).

In Genesis we find that man and animals were told to eat only plants (Genesis 1:29, 30); they were vegetarians. Only after the Flood was man told he could eat meat (Genesis 9:3). They were only vegetarians when God first created, and there was no violence before Adam sinned. Some people object to the claim that the first creatures were vegetarian by saying that lions have sharp teeth which were created to eat meat. Is that necessarily so? Or is that just what you were taught in school? What we should say is that the lion's sharp, canine teeth are good for ripping. The same teeth that are now good for ripping up other animals would also be good for ripping up plants. According to God's Word, lions were vegetarian before the Fall and will be once again in the future paradise. By the way, "meat-eating" animals can still be vegetarian. Dogs and cats will survive quite well on a balanced diet of vegetables. Also, the Bible does not exclude the possibility of direct action by God at the time of the Fall (and in the future restoration), having a direct biological effect on the creatures in relation to feeding habits. There are many animals living today that have carnivorous-looking teeth (e.g., the flying fox or fruit bat), but they only use these teeth for eating fruit or plants (See Appendix 1).

To believe in evolution is to deny a universal paradise before Adam, because evolution necessarily implies that before Adam there was struggle, cruelty and brutality, animals eating animals, and death. Is the world going to be restored to that? If you believe in evolution, you must deny a universal paradise before Adam (because you believe that there was death and struggle millions of years before Adam), and also at the end of time (because the Bible teaches the world will be restored to what it used to be). Thus, evolution not only strikes at the heart and the foundation, but at the hope of Christianity as well. We all should be out there doing something about it. Many of us have been hoodwinked into thinking that evolution has to do with science and that you need to be a scientist to do anything to combat it. But evolution is only a belief system, and you do not need to be a scientist to combat that.

Also, Christians who do believe in evolution must accept that evolution is still going on. This is because the death and struggle we see in the world around us and the mutations (mistakes in the genes) that are occurring are used by evolutionists to try to prove that evolution is possible. They extrapolate into the past what they see today, and deduce that these processes over millions of years are the basis for evolution. Christians who accept evolution must agree, therefore, that evolution is occurring today in every area, including man. However, God has said in His Word that when He created everything He finished His work of creation and pronounced it "good" (Genesis 1:31-2:3). This is completely contrary to what evolutionists are telling us. Theistic evolutionists cannot say that God once used evolution and now does not. To say that evolution is not occurring today is to destroy evolutionary theory, as you have no basis for saying it ever happened in the past.

There are many Christians who, after being taught the true nature of science—that evolution is religion—abandon beliefs such as theistic evolution and progressive creation. However, there are a number of ministers, theologians, and others who, because of their whole view of Scripture, will not accept what we are saying. They have a basic philosophical disagreement with us in regard to how to approach the Bible.

Perhaps the best way to summarize this argument is to give you a practical example from an encounter I had with a Protestant church minister.

Personnel from the Creation Science Foundation in Brisbane, Australia, had travelled 1700 kilometers to Victoria to conduct meetings in various centers. In one location, this minister opposed us publicly. Another minister, in the same church, had put an advertisement in the church's weekly announcement sheet concerning our visit. The opposing minister obtained the stencil before the announcement sheet was printed and deleted the advertisement. He encouraged people to boycott our seminar program and made many discouraging public statements concerning our organization and teachings. He even told people that we were of the devil and they should not listen to us.

I made an appointment to see this minister to discuss the issue with him. He explained that he believed Genesis was only symbolic, that there were a great many mistakes in the Bible and one could not take it as literally as I appeared to do. The reason we had this disagreement concerning creation/evolution was because we had a basic philosophical disagreement regarding our personal approach to the Scriptures. He agreed this was so, but again emphasized one could not take Genesis literally and that it was only symbolic. I asked him whether he believed that God created the heavens and the earth.

He said, "Yes, this was the message that Genesis was teaching."

Deliberately, I quoted Genesis 1:1, "Do you believe, 'In the beginning God created the heavens and the earth'?"

He said, "Yes, of course I do. That is the message Genesis is getting across to us."

I explained to him that he had just taken Genesis 1:1 literally. He was asked whether Genesis 1:1 was symbolic, and, if not, why did he take it literally. I then asked whether Genesis 1:2 was literal or symbolic. I pointed out the inconsistency of accepting Genesis 1:1 as literal but saying the whole of Genesis was symbolic. He went on to say it was not important what Genesis said—only what it meant was important.

"How can you ever understand the meaning of anything if you do not know what it says?" I asked. "If you cannot take what it says to arrive at the meaning, then the English (or any other) language really becomes nonsense."

I then asked him how he decided what was truth concerning the Scriptures. He replied, "By a consensus of opinion amongst the fellowship."

So I said, "This then is your basis for deciding what truth is. Where did you get this basis from, and how do you know that this is the right basis for deciding truth?"

He looked at me and said, "By a consensus of opinion amongst scholars."

I again posed the question to him, "If this now is your basis for deciding truth and determining whether or not your fellowship has come to the right conclusions about truth, how do you know that this is the right basis to determine what truth is?"

He then told me that he did not have all day to talk about this topic, and it was best we now finish the discussion. What he was doing, of course, was appealing to man's wisdom to decide what Scripture meant or said, rather than allowing God's Word to tell him what the truth was. The real difference between our positions could be summed up as follows: **Where do you put your faith—in the words of men who are fallible creatures who do not know everything, who were not there—or the Words of God who is perfect, who knows everything, and who was there?**

Christians (or those claiming to be Christian) who take this liberal view of Scripture will more often than not see the outworkings of this wrong philosophy in the next generation: their children. Because they cannot provide a solid foundation for their children, they frequently see the whole structure of Christianity collapsing in the next generation. For many of these people, it is sad but true that most of their children will reject Christianity completely. This dilemma in regard to liberal theology is very much related to the controversy concerning Genesis. If one rejects Genesis, or claims it is only symbolism or myth, this logically leads to a denial of the rest of Scripture. You see this reflected in people who try to explain away the miracles, such as the crossing of the Red Sea, the burning bush, or a fish swallowing a man (to name but a few). But, these people do not stop there. They go on to explain away the miracles of Christ in the New Testament. Sometimes (and increasingly so), even the virgin birth and the resurrection are denied. Once one accepts Genesis as literal and understands it as foundational for the rest of Scripture, it is an easy step to accepting as truth the remainder of what the Bible says. I take the Bible literally unless it is obviously symbolic. Even where it is symbolic, the words and phrases used have a literal basis.

Many people use the example in Scripture where it says that Jesus is the Door to say that we cannot take that literally. However, understanding the customs of the times, we find that the shepherd used to sit in the gate and literally be the door. So, in this sense, Jesus is literally the door, just as the shepherd literally was the door. Too many people are quick to jump to conclusions concerning the literalness of Scripture without carefully considering the statement, the context and the customs. When Scripture is meant to be taken symbolically or metaphorically, it is either obviously so from the context or we are told so.

Of course, many liberal theologians claim that the creation ministry is divisive. In that claim they certainly are correct; the truth always divides. As Christ said, He came with a sword to divide, "For I am come to set a man at variance against his father, and the daughter against her mother, and the daughter-in-law against her mother-in-law" (Matthew 10:35, KJV). How many situations do you know where relationships have been broken because of the tension between living as a Christian and not living as one? Compromise is too often made with the Christian giving ground for the sake of peace and harmony. Jesus predicted strife, not peace at any price. In Luke 12:51 (KJV) Jesus said, "Suppose ye that I am come to give peace on earth? I tell you, Nay: but rather division" (See also John 7:12, 43; 9:16; 10:19).

From a practical perspective, I find that students do not want somebody telling them the Bible is full of mistakes or that they cannot believe it. They want to hear that there are answers and that they can really know.

At one meeting a mother told me that her daughter was in the class I had spoken to at the local public school. Her daughter had told her that the thing that impressed the students more than anything was the fact that I spoke with such authority. They were impressed that I did not question God's Word, but totally accepted it. It reminded me of the statement in the Scriptures: "The people were astonished at His doctrine: for He taught them as one having authority, and not as the scribes" (Matthew 7:28, 29, KJV). Jesus was very authoritative and very dogmatic in the way He spoke. He did not preach various ways into heaven. He did not come and say that He believed He was one of the ways to eternal life. Jesus said, "I am **the** Way, **the** Truth and **the** Life" (John 14:6, KJV). I do not think Jesus would be accepted in many churches today if He were to preach. He would be too divisive! It was little different two thousand years ago. Are we, as born-again Christians, who are the embodiment of Christ on earth today, too scared to proclaim the truth in case we are divisive?

I spoke to one particular church youth group on the importance of Genesis. I was amazed at the youth leader, who, at the end of the program, told the young people how disappointed he was with my "low" view of Scripture. He said that I was trying to impose a perfect Bible on God and how inadequate this view of Scripture was.

They, on the other hand, were prepared to accept that there were mistakes and problems in the Bible. This led to a very "high" view of Scripture. After this conversation, I decided that words were meaningless for this person.

Many people (particularly those of the younger generation) have commented on the dearth of authoritative teaching. It is a sad indictment upon our churches. What are they feeding their people?

CHAPTER 8

The Evils of Evolution

The following diagram and comments summarize thus far what has been said.

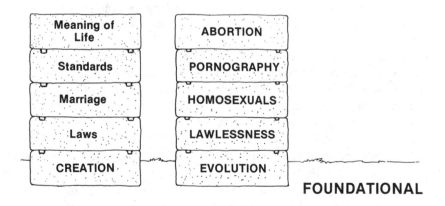

If you accept a belief in God as Creator, then you accept that there are laws, since He is the Lawgiver. God's Law is the reflection of His holy character. He is the Absolute Authority, and we are under total obligation to Him. Laws are not a matter of our opinions but rules given by the One who has the right to impose them upon us for our good, and His own glory. He gives us principles as a basis for building our thinking in every area.

Accepting the God of Creation tells us what life is all about. We know that God is the Lifegiver. We know that life has meaning and purpose, and we know that all humans are created in the image of God and, therefore, are of great value and significance. **God made us so that He could relate to us, love us and pour out His blessing on us, and so that we could love Him in return.**

On the other hand, if you reject God and replace Him with another belief that puts chance, random processes in the place of God, there is no basis for right or wrong. Rules become whatever you want to make them. There are no absolutes—no principles that must be adhered to. People will write their own rules.

It must be understood that our world-view is inevitably affected by what we believe concerning *our origins and our destiny*.

As the creation foundation is removed, we see the Godly institutions also start to collapse. On the other hand, as the evolution foundation remains firm, the structures built on that foundation—lawlessness, homosexuality, abortion, etc., logically increase. We must understand this connection.

Many Christians recognize the degeneration that has occurred in society. They see the collapse in Christian ethics and the increase in anti-God philosophies. They are well aware of the increase in lawlessness, homosexuality, pornography, and abortion (and other products of humanistic philosophy), but they are at a loss to know why this is occurring. The reason they are in such a dilemma is that they do not understand the foundational nature of the battle. Creation versus evolution is the bottom line.

If you find it hard to believe that evolution is related to the above issues, some basic research into history will demonstrate the connection clearly. In fact, I have not yet met one informed evolutionist who has disagreed with me concerning the relationship of evolution to these particular moral issues. They might not necessarily agree that this should have happened, but they do agree that this is the way in which people have applied evolution. It is important that you do not misunderstand what I am saying at this point. Certainly, evil, anti-God philosophies have existed before Darwinian evolution. People aborted babies before Darwin popularized his view of evolution. However, what people believe about where they came from does affect their world view. When people reject the God of creation, it affects how they view themselves, others, and the world in which they live.

Particularly in the Western nations, where Christian ethics were once very prevalent, Darwinian evolution provided a justification for people not to believe in God and, therefore, to do those things which Christians would deem as wrong. As one non-Christian scientist said in a TV interview, "Darwinian evolution helped make atheism respectable."

We are now going to consider a number of areas where evolution has been used to justify people's attitudes and actions. This does not mean that Darwinian evolution is the cause of these attitudes or actions but rather has been used by people as a justification to make their particular philosophy "respectable" in their eyes. These are covered in more detail and documented in Dr. Henry Morris' book, *Creation and the Modern Christian*. (See the list of resources at the end of this book for details.)

1. Nazism and Evolution

Much has been written about one of Fascism's more infamous sons, Adolf Hitler. His treatment of the Jews may be attributed, at least in part, to his belief in evolution. P. Hoffman, in *Hitler's Personal Security* (Pergamon, 1979, p. 264), said: "Hitler believed in struggle as a Darwinian principle of human life that forced every people to try to dominate all others; without struggle they would rot and perish . . . . Even in his own defeat in April 1945, Hitler expressed his faith in the survival of the stronger and declared the Slavic peoples to have proven themselves the stronger."

Sir Arthur Keith, the well-known evolutionist, explains how Hitler was only being consistent in what he did to the Jews—he was applying the principles of Darwinian evolution. In *Evolution and Ethics* (New York, Putnam, 1947, p. 28), he said: "To see evolutionary measures and tribal morality being applied vigorously to the affairs of a great modern nation, we must turn again to Germany of 1942. We see Hitler devoutly convinced that evolution produces the only real basis for a national policy . . . . The means he adopted to secure the destiny of his race and people were organized slaughter, which has drenched Europe in blood . . . . Such conduct is highly immoral as measured by every scale of ethics, yet Germany justifies it; it is consonant with tribal or evolutionary morality. Germany has reverted to the tribal past, and is demonstrating to the world, in their naked ferocity, the methods of evolution."

2. Racism and Evolution

Stephen J. Gould in *Natural History* (April 1980, p. 144), said that "Recapitulation [the evolutionary theory which postulates that a developing embryo in its mother's womb goes through evolutionary stages, such as the fish stage, etc., until it becomes human] provided a convenient focus for the pervasive racism of white scientists; they looked to the activities of their own children for comparison with normal, adult behavior in lower races" (brackets mine). Gould also concludes that the term "mongoloid" became synonymous with mentally defective people because it was believed the Caucasian race was more highly developed than the Mongoloid. Therefore, some thought that a mentally defective child was really a throwback to a previous stage in evolution. The leading American paleontologist of the first half of the twentieth century, Henry Fairfield Osborne, adds fuel to the fire with his belief that "The Negroid stock is even more ancient than the Caucasian and Mongolian . . . . The standard of intelligence of the average adult Negro is similar to that of the eleven-year-old of the species Homo sapiens" (*Natural History*, April 1980, p. 129).

Many of the early settlers of Australia considered the Australian Aborigines to be less intelligent than the "white man," because aborigines had not evolved as far as whites on the evolutionary scale. In fact, the Hobart Museum in Tasmania (Australia) in 1984 listed this as one of the reasons why early white settlers killed as many aborigines as they could in that state. In 1924, the *New York Tribune* (Sunday, February 10) had a very large article telling their readers that the missing link had been found in Australia. The missing link referred to happened to be aborigines from the State of Tasmania.[1]

---

[1] The evolutionary thinking that has influenced people's attitude to the Tasmanian Aborigines has been well documented in various museum publications and other material. Full details may be obtained by writing to the author.

The incredible thing is that we live in a society that states it wants to be rid of racist attitudes. Yet we are conditioned to racist attitudes by our very education system, and the whole foundational basis for racism permeates people's minds.

It was the evolutionary view that convinced anthropologists there were different races of humans at different levels on the evolutionary ladder. This led them to believe there were different levels of intelligence and ability. It is the Christian view that teaches there is one race (in the sense that we all came from the same two humans, and therefore there are no lower or higher evolutionary groups) and that all people are equal.

At one school, a teacher said to her students that, if ape-like creatures had evolved into people, then this should be seen to be happening today. Some of the students told her that this was happening today because some aborigines are primitive and therefore, still evolving. Regrettably, in the children's eyes the teaching of evolution had relegated the Australian Aborigines to a subhuman level.

3. Drugs and Evolution

Many people would not think of evolution as being in any way related to the taking of drugs. However, the following letter of testimony from a man in Western Australia shows clearly this relationship.

"At School, the theory of evolution was presented in such a way that none of us ever doubted it was scientific fact. Although the school was supposedly Christian, the Biblical account of creation was presented as a kind of romantic fiction, not intended to convey literal truths about God, man or the cosmos. As a result, I assumed the Bible was unscientific, and therefore practically of little or no use.

"It never occurred to me that evolution was only an assumption—a concept concocted in someone's head—and I regret to say that I wasn't sufficiently interested to go check out the so-called 'facts' for myself. I assumed that reliable people had already done that.

"After I left school, I began to put into practice the assumptions and presuppositions I'd picked up during childhood. My naive belief in evolution had three important practical consequences:

"1. It strongly encouraged me to look to drugs as an ultimate source of comfort and creativity.

"2. It led me to the conclusion that God, if He was around at all, was a very distant and impersonal figure, separated from humanity by very great distances of space and time.

"3. It led me to increasingly abandon the moral values I had been taught at home, because when man is viewed as an arbitrary by-product of Time + Matter + Chance, there is no logical reason for treating men or women as objects of dignity and respect, since in principle they are no different from the animals, trees, and rocks from which they supposedly came.

"I want to elaborate on just one point, the great faith in dope that I had as a result of being convinced that evolution was 'fact.' After leaving school, I became increasingly susceptible to drugs. Drug-taking seemed to me to make sense, because in principle it fitted with what I'd been taught about the nature and origin of man. 'From chemical reactions hast thou come, and unto chemicals thou shalt return.' And so I did.

"My faith in drugs as a source of comfort and creativity was almost unbreakable even after ten years of total devastation, during which my job, personality and relationships had fallen apart. Even after I came to Christ, I still continued using drugs, or feeling strongly drawn to using them, until some Christians had pointed out the truth about man's nature, origin and destiny as recounted in Genesis. It was only when I perceived the truth of this, that my private love of drugs was completely and voluntarily abandoned. **I now know that my hope is in the Person of Jesus Christ, and in Him only. It's no longer a platitude, but a living reality. I'm free, and it is the truth which has made me free—free even from any desires for dope, free from the compelling faith I once had in chemicals as a result of believing in a lie—the lie of evolution.** I appeal to you parents and teachers, to reexamine the evidence as I have done."

4. Abortion and Evolution

Many will remember being taught at school that as an embryo develops in its mother's womb it goes through a fish stage with gill slits, etc., and other evolutionary stages until it becomes human. In other words, the idea is that as the embryo develops it passes through all the evolutionary stages reflecting its ancestry. This theory of "embryonic recapitulation" was first proposed by a man called Ernst Haeckel. Not many people realize that this whole theory was an intentional deception. I quote, "But it still remains true that, in attempting to prove his law, Haeckel resorted to a series of dishonest distortions in making his illustrations. Branding them as dishonest is not too harsh, since Haeckel mentions where he originally procured some of his drawings without mentioning the alterations he made" (*Creation Research Society 1969 Annual*, Volume 6, Number 1, June 1969, p. 28).

Eventually, Ernst Haeckel admitted this fraud, but the deplorable aspect is that this theory is still taught in many universities, schools and colleges throughout the world. Admittedly, evolutionists who have kept up with the latest writings know that this view is wrong and refrain from teaching it in their classes. However, in most of the popular school textbooks and reading materials this view is still promulgated in various forms, often very subtly.

As people accepted that the child developing in a mother's womb was just an animal reflecting its evolutionary ancestry, there was less and less problem about destroying it. As evolutionary ideas became more accepted, the easier it became to accept abortion. In fact, some abortion clinics in America have taken women aside to explain to them that what is being aborted is just an embryo in the fish stage of evolution, and that the embryo must not be thought of as human. These women are being fed outright lies.

Again, let me state here that abortion certainly existed before Darwin popularized his evolutionary theory. However, his evolutionary theory has been used to give abortion its respectability, and thus the great increase in abortion that we see today.

5. Business Methods and Evolution

In the last half of the nineteenth century, a widespread philosophy known as "social Darwinism" dominated the thinking of many industrial tycoons of the era. They believed that because evolution was true in the biological sphere, the same methods should apply in the business world: survival of the fittest, elimination of the weak, no love for the poor.

In 1985 one of Australia's large banks (the National Australia Bank) in a commemorative magazine concerning their merging with another bank, was using Darwinian principles of survival of the fittest to justify its merger. There are many other examples in the history books of famous business men who have accepted evolutionism and applied it in the business field.

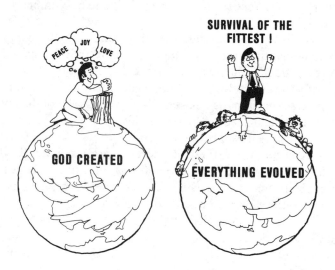

6. Male Chauvinism and Evolution

Many try to blame Christianity for the chauvinist attitude of many males in our society. They claim the Bible teaches that men are superior to women and that women are not equal to men. This, of course, is not true. The Bible teaches that men and women are equal, but they have different roles because of the way God created them and because of their reactions to the temptation of the serpent (I Timothy 2:12-14). In *New Scientist* (Volume 100, December 22/29, 1983, p. 887), Eveleen Richards states: "In a period when women were beginning to demand the suffrage, higher education and entrance to middle-class professions, it was comforting to know that women could never outstrip men; the new Darwinism scientifically guaranteed it." She went on in the article to say: " . . . an evolutionary reconstruction that centers on the aggressive, territorial, hunting male and relegates the female to submissive domesticity and the periphery of the evolutionary process." In other words, some have used Darwinian evolution to justify that females are inferior. However, there are those in the feminist movement today who use evolution to try to justify that females are superior. There are even those who use evolution to justify children's rights. When you think about this, any theory that justifies either male or female supremacy justifies neither.

Christian women need to realize that the radical feminist movement is pervaded by evolutionist philosophy. Christian women need to be alert and not be deceived by such an anti-God movement.

A whole book could be written about the justification of many of the evils we see today from a foundational acceptance of evolutionary philosophy. But at this stage people start saying to me, "Are you blaming evolution for all the evils in society?" My answer is, "Yes and no." No—because it is not primarily evolution that is to blame, but the rejection of God as Creator. As people reject the God of Creation and therefore reject His rules, they abandon Christian ethics and accept beliefs in accordance with their own opinions. Yes—because, in a very real sense, the justification for people rejecting the God of creation is the so-called "scientific" view of evolution. Evolution is the main justification today for rejecting belief in divine creation.

The following illustration is my favorite and beautifully summarizes what this book is all about.

On the left we see the foundation of evolution. The castle built upon it is entitled "humanism." Associated with the humanist structure are the issues we have been discussing. On the right we see the foundation of creation, and built upon that is the castle entitled "Christianity." As part of the foundation collapses, the structure starts to collapse.

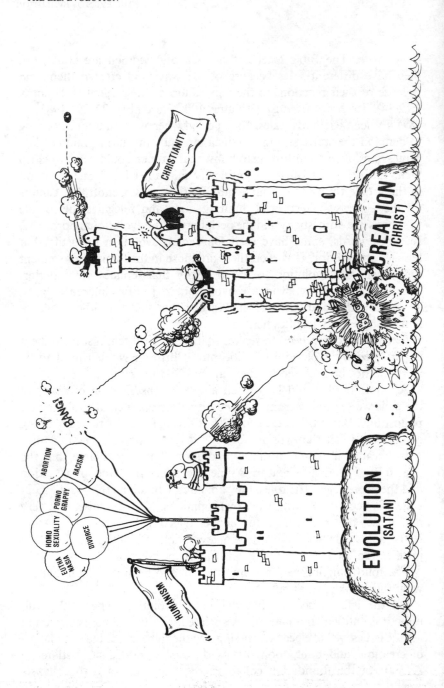

However, on the Christian structure, the cannons are either aimed at each other, aimed nowhere, or aimed at the issues of humanism, but certainly not aimed at the foundation called evolution.

Christians are fighting a war, but they don't know where to fight it or how to aim their guns. This is the real problem. If we want to see the structure of humanism collapse (which any thinking Christian must), then we have to reaim the cannons at the foundation of evolution. It is only when the foundation is destroyed that the structure will collapse.

You will notice that one cannon is taking pot-shots at the issues of humanism represented as balloons. Here is another aspect that Christians must consider very carefully. Many might even agree to fight against such issues as abortion, sexual immorality, pornography, and so on. But if we attack only at the level of these issues and not the motivation for their popularity, we are not going to be successful. Even if the laws are changed in our society to outlaw abortion, but the reason abortion has become acceptable (evolution) has not been attacked or destroyed, the next generation will be even more conditioned to evolution and simply change the law again. If the church wants to be successful in changing society's attitudes toward abortion, pornography and homosexuality, it is going to have to fight the issue at a foundational level. The foundational basis of evolution needs to be destroyed and the foundational basis of creation restored to its rightful place of importance.

Another way of summing up what is happening is seen in the following illustration.

You can see in this diagram that the boat "Christianity" has had its hull "SS Creation" holed by torpedoes of "Evolution" from the submarine "Humanism." Notice the ship, "Christianity." The Christians are looking around and endeavoring to discover why the boat is sinking. They are bailing hard, but the boat is sinking faster than they can actually bail. Their mistake lies in not realizing the subversive nature of the attack—the ship's "foundations" are being shot to pieces.

Dear reader, there is a war raging. We are soldiers of the King. It is our responsibility to be out their fighting for the King of Kings and Lord of Lords. We are the King's army. But are we using the right weapons? Are we fighting the battle where it really matters? Unfortunately, many Christians have what would be viewed militarily

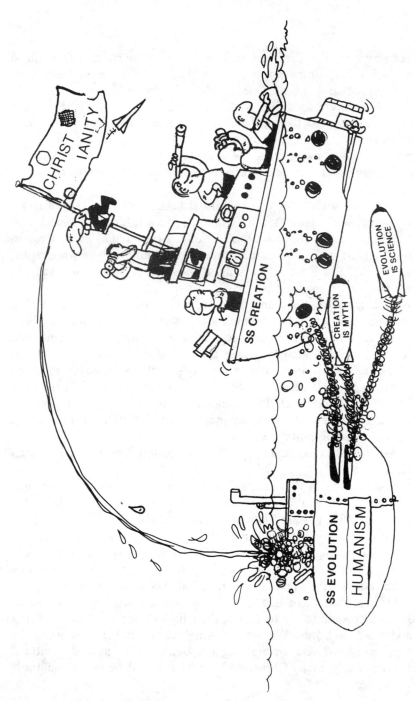

as a totally ridiculous strategy. They do not fight the battle where it rages. They are not fighting on the real battleground. They have no hope of winning. When are Christians in the nations around our world going to wake up to the fact that we need to re-aim our weapons and aggressively and actively fight the issue of evolution by restoring the foundation of Creation?

In Western nations most churches compromise with evolution. Many theological and Bible colleges teach that the issue of creation/evolution does not matter. They teach that you can believe in both evolution and the Bible because you do not have to bother about taking Genesis literally. This compromising stand is helping to destroy the very structure they claim to want to remain in society—the structure of Christianity. Chapter 10 challenges all those involved in pastoral and teaching positions in our churches to take a positive stand for the God of Creation and thus oppose the anti-God philosophies that are destroying our nations.

CHAPTER 9

Evangelism in a Pagan World

There is a war going on in society—a very real battle. The war is Christianity versus humanism, but we must wake up to the fact that, at the foundational level, it's really creation versus evolution.

Having agreed on all this, however, we must remember that our enemies are not the humanists and evolutionists themselves, but the powers of darkness that have deceived them. We must demonstrate grace toward humanists and evolutionists and let them see clearly in us the fruits of the Spirit—in all we say, write and do.

When Christians understand the foundational nature of the battle, it is a key that unlocks for them the reasons for the happenings in society. It is also a key to unlock an approach to society enabling us to combat its increasingly anti-Christian emphasis.

It wasn't so very long ago that Biblical creation was the basis of our society. Creation was taught in the universities and the school system. People automatically sent their children to Sunday School or similar places, so they would learn Christian absolutes. Even people who were not Christians, by and large, respected and obeyed these laws based upon the Bible. Sexual deviancy in all areas was outlawed. Abortion in most instances was considered murder.

But, what happened? Charles Darwin popularized the theory of evolution. (There have always been evolutionary views opposing the true record of creation. Darwin did not originate the idea of evolution— he just popularized a particular version of it.) Evolution was promoted as science, but it is not science—it is a belief system about the past. The church was caught off guard because it did not know how to handle the situation. Because they did not understand the true nature of science, many people believed that Darwinian evolution was science. And so this view of origins began to permeate our society.

Atheistic evolution is a belief system that says there is no God. We are a result of chance. No one owns us; we own ourselves. Non-Christians easily accept this view because the Bible tells us that men love darkness rather than light, as they are sinful creatures (John 3:19).

As stated in the previous chapter, the clash we see in our society at present is the clash between the religion of Christianity with its creation basis (and therefore absolutes) and the religion of humanism with its evolutionary basis and its relative morality that says "anything goes." What can we do about it? We must preach the Gospel. This means teaching the whole counsel of God to ensure that Jesus Christ is given the glory due to His Name. But what is the Gospel? Many don't really understand the full substance of the Gospel. This Gospel consists of:

1. The foundational teachings: Jesus Christ is Creator and He made man; Man rebelled against God, and sin therefore entered the world; God placed upon man the curse of death.

2. The power of the Gospel and what is central to the Gospel: Jesus Christ, the Creator, came and suffered the same curse of death on a cross and was raised from the dead (thus conquering death); All those who come to Him in repentance for their sin (rebellion) can come back to the perfect love relationship with God that was forfeited in the Garden of Eden.

3. The hope of the Gospel: the whole of creation is suffering the effects of sin and is slowly running down; All things are to be restored (the consummation of all things) when Jesus Christ comes to complete His work of redemption and reconciliation (Colossians 1; II Peter 3).

Many people use I Corinthians 15 as a passage that defines the Gospel and claim that this only talks about Jesus Christ being crucified and raised from the dead. However, in I Corinthians 15:12-14 (KJV) Paul says: "Now if Christ be preached that He rose from the dead, how say some among you that there is no resurrection of the dead? But if there be no resurrection of the dead, then is Christ not risen:

and if Christ be not risen, then is our preaching vain, and your faith is also vain." In other words, Paul is talking about the people who do not believe the resurrection. But now have a look at the tack Paul takes. In verse 21, he goes back to Genesis and explains the origin of sin. "For since by man came death, by man came also the resurrection of the dead" (KJV). He sets the foundational reason as to why Jesus Christ came and died on the cross. It is important to realize that the Gospel consists of the foundational aspects as well as the other elements as outlined above. Therefore, to preach the Gospel without the message of Christ as Creator and the entrance of sin and death is to preach a Gospel without a foundation. To preach a Gospel without the message of Christ and His crucifixion and resurrection is to preach a Gospel without power. To preach a Gospel without the message of the coming kingdom is to preach a Gospel without hope. All these aspects constitute the Gospel. Therefore, to understand the Gospel message properly we must understand all aspects.

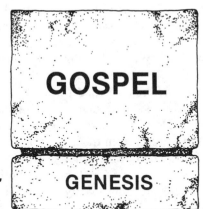

FOUNDATIONAL KNOWLEDGE

Methods of Evangelism

Many Christians feel that it is sufficient to preach concerning the death of Christ for our sin, the need for repentance, and the receiving of Christ as Savior, leaving the outworking to the Holy Spirit. However, it is quite evident that the early church evangelists used different presentations according to the people they found before them. Examples abound in Acts and the Gospels:

John 4—Jesus used the "living water" approach at the well.

Acts 2—Peter used the explanation of the circumstances of the Day of Pentecost as a starting point.

Acts 3—Peter used the healing of the lame man to speak of God's power.

Acts 7—Stephen gave a history lesson to the Sanhedrin.

Acts 13—Paul preached Jesus as the Christ in the synagogue.

Acts 14 & 17—Paul preached the **Creator God** to the Gentiles.

The Lord has raised up creation ministries world-wide so that all necessary methods for evangelizing our society will be available. The Lord has provided us with a phenomenally powerful tool that must be used today—**creation evangelism.** The main reason, we believe, that the church is so relatively ineffective is a direct result of not evangelizing correctly. The church is proclaiming the message of the cross and Christ, but it is not as effective as it used to be. We also read in the New Testament (I Corinthians 1:23) that the preaching of the cross was foolishness to the Gentiles (Greeks), but only a stumbling block to the Jews. We need to take a lesson from the New Testament. In Acts 14 and 17, we are given two specific approaches to the Greeks. It was a different method from that used for the Jews. When Paul went to the Greeks, he didn't start preaching about Jesus Christ and the cross. He commenced by telling them about the true God who is the Creator, and from there went on to the rest of the Gospel about Jesus Christ. The Greeks believed in a form of evolution and, in their eyes, there was no one Creator God who had authority over them.

There are only two types of views about origins: evolutionary or creationist. If one does not believe that there is an Infinite Being who created all, the only alternative is that some form of evolution must apply.

When we think about this very carefully, we can begin to understand why Paul needed to approach the Greeks on the basis of creation. The Greeks, who did not believe in God as Creator but rather a form of evolution, had the wrong basis and, therefore, the wrong framework of thinking about this world. Consequently, to them the preaching of the cross was utter foolishness. Paul realized that before he could preach about Jesus Christ he had to establish the basis upon which he could build the rest of the Gospel. So, he established creation as a foundation and from there preached the message of Jesus Christ.

Whenever the Jews were approached, it was not with the message of creation first, but the teaching of Christ and the cross. The Jews already had the right foundation because they believed in God as Creator; therefore, they had the right framework of thinking. Even so, many refused to accept who Jesus was.

It's about time the modern church came to grips with a society that is more "Greek" than "Jewish" in outlook. In fact, the modern church itself is largely more "Greek" than "Jewish." Whereas, in the past, the creation basis was evident in society and people were less ignorant of Christian doctrine, late Twentieth Century man knows little of that. We have to come to grips with the fact that evolution has become one of the biggest barriers to today's people being receptive to the Gospel of Jesus Christ. We have many letters from people indicating that they would not listen to the claims of Christianity because they thought evolution had proved it to be wrong.

We must appreciate that there are whole generations of students coming through an educational system who know nothing of the Bible. They have never heard about creation, Noah's Flood, or the message of the cross. It is hard to believe that there are literally millions of people in Western society who don't have this background, but it is becoming increasingly obvious.

When I was working at the office of the Creation Science Foundation in Brisbane, Australia, we rang a florist to send one of my secretaries a bouquet of flowers to cheer her up. The young girl on the other end of the phone was told three times, in very clear English, what to write on the card to be delivered with the flowers: John 14 verse 27. When the card arrived, the girl had handwritten the following message, "John 14 birth 27." This young woman had no understanding of the Bible or Christianity and so did not have any idea what that request was all about. My secretary was able to decipher the message easily enough (she knows the verse by heart) and was somewhat cheered by the strange presentation. This is a humorous but sad reflection on what so many young people of today are becoming.

In an increasing number of instances, it is apparent that before we can effectively proclaim the message of Christ we must establish the

creation foundation upon which the rest of the Gospel can be built.

Let me be emphatic here. The doctrine of the cross, though regarded as absurd and powerless by non-Christians, has more power and wisdom than anything that ever proceeded from man. The preaching of this doctrine is the great means of salvation. To this all other teachings, however important, are either preparatory or subordinate. The doctrine of Christ crucified produces effects that nothing short of divine power can accomplish. So, in saying that we need to start from the foundational basis of creation, I am not detracting from the message of the cross. What I am attempting to show is that there is a particular method of approach that is necessary when presenting the Gospel message to certain people. The beliefs that they hold can be barriers to their even listening when you preach the message of the cross.

Perhaps, too, we should rethink the method prevalent in Christian circles of handing unbelievers numerous copies of the New Testament, Psalms and Proverbs. If they were directed to Genesis 1 through 11, as well as the New Testament, the basis would be provided for the Gospel presentation in the same sense as Paul used it in Acts 14 and 17. We believe there would be greater effectiveness in the lives of those who read these Bible portions—a greater preparedness to accept the whole of the Word of God as truthful and inerrant.

Evolution as a barrier can also be seen in Moslem countries. On one occasion, I was speaking to a Christian Egyptian who told me that Islam is a creation-based religion, but the teaching of evolution in schools in Egypt caused many young people to totally reject this religion. It is interesting to see that another creation-based religion has the same problem with evolution. This should make it even more obvious to Christians that evolution is a barrier to people believing in a Creator God.

I have seen this problem in the public school system. Students would often say such things as, "Sir, how can you believe the Bible is true when it says God created Adam and Eve? We know that has been proved wrong by science." Evolution, I believe, is one of the biggest barriers to people today being receptive to the Gospel of Jesus Christ. Many people (who previously would not consider Christianity) have come to listen to the message of Christianity after these barriers were removed.

For example, a high school student wrote, "I thank God for the

Creation Science visit to our senior high school. The information was up to date, relevant and created much discussion. After the seminar various students said they believed what was said. Certainly they felt the speaker made more sense about how everything began than much they had heard at the school. Without the visit of Creation Science many people would still regard the evolution lie as a fact. Many students, who used to believe in evolution, now believe the Genesis account thanks to Creation Science. Creation Science has a great mission field and a great role to play in schools. It's up to individuals like me to continue to be faithful to the message they bring and extend the great work done."

This student also said that as a result of the visit, students who previously scoffed at him for being a Christian were now interested in finding out more about the Creator. I have heard this testimony many, many times during my years in the creation evangelism ministry.

If God's people do not take up the tool of creation evangelism and use it, we will suffer the consequences of an ineffective method of proclaiming the truth. This is why creation ministries are so important today. They deal with the foundations upon which Christianity depends—the foundations that have been removed to a great extent from our society.

As this message has been preached throughout Australia, the United States, and other places around the world, we have seen people take the thoughts and publications and challenge others in the area of creation. When confronted on that issue, they have been found to be open to the Gospel, whereas previously they would just scoff when the subject of Christ was raised. By the grace of God, creation evangelism works!

When new converts come into a church, they should be led in a Bible study on the book of Genesis. They will learn exactly what Christianity is all about and will learn the basis for all Christian doctrine. Results do come from simply preaching about Christ and the cross in our society today, because there is still a remnant of the Creation basis for that preaching. But this remnant is disappearing very quickly, and thus the response is far less today than in the past. It is time we woke up and used the tools that the Lord has provided to evangelize a society that has become like the ancient Greeks. It is time to restore the foundations of Christianity.

A good example of creation evangelism at work can be summarized in the letter we received from an excited young university student:

"I would like to thank you for your ministry as you help people understand that Jesus actually created this world.

"I want to share a testimony which I pray will encourage you in your fight against evolution.

"My father for sixty-five years had been an atheist, always had been an atheist, always quick to knock down anyone's beliefs concerning God in general, but especially if they claimed that God had made the world. Dad thought the Bible was illogical and a book for the simple in mind. 'How could it contain any truth?' he questioned. Dad assumed that evolution was the only possible scientific way to explain the formation of the earth.

"Sensing this spiritual attack, my faithful mother prayed for twenty years for Dad's mind to open to the truth and for this deception to be broken. Two years ago, when I was eighteen and had been a Christian for three years, I decided to go to a Creation Science seminar. I can't tell you how impressed I was with these Bible-believing Christians presenting scientific truth about creation. It made my faith in God's Word increasingly stronger and I was overjoyed that I could take a scientific stand to explain how God created the world.

"At the book-stand at the seminar I bought several books and magazines. One in particular was *Bone of Contention*. I loved reading this magazine so much that I encouraged Dad to read it. Skeptically, he took it and started reading it. Three days after, I asked him what he thought about it. To my surprise he stated that it really made him think. At this opening I then proceeded to give him the other books I had bought.

"A few weeks later Dad was making statements like "never knew there were so many holes in the evolutionary theory. There must have been an Almighty Being who created the world." Each new day Jesus began to piece together the puzzle in Dad's mind concerning creation and the claim of Jesus on his life. A few weeks later an evangelist came to our church. The same night Dad decided to go. The evangelist spoke on creation versus evolution. God's timing is perfect! That night

Dad accepted Jesus Christ into his heart as his personal Savior!!
I praise God that He can take a lost soul off the highway
to hell and set him on the path to life simply because an
understanding of how God created the world was formed in
his mind!

"Thanks, Creation Science, for teaching people about
creation. I want to encourage you in your fight against Satan.
The Lord is doing wonderful things as a result of your effort."

The Lord has not just called us to tear down the barrier of evolution,
but to help to restore the foundation of the Gospel in our society.
If churches took up the tool of creation evangelism in society we would
see a stemming of the tide of humanistic philosophy, which is making
our nations more pagan with each passing day.

In Australia's Christian newspaper, *New Life*, Thursday, April 15,
1982, Josef Ton, who was a pastor of the largest Baptist Church in
Romania and is now living in exile in the United States, stated: "I
came to the conclusion that there were two factors which destroyed
Christianity in Western Europe. One was the theory of evolution, and
the other, liberal theology . . . . Liberal theology is just evolution
applied to the Bible and our faith."

It is also worth noting the comment in the book, *By Their Blood:
Christian Martyrs of the 20th Century* by James and Marti Helfley
(Mott Media, pp. 49, 50): "New philosophies and theologies from the
West also helped to erode Chinese confidence in Christianity. A new
wave of so-called missionaries from mainline Protestant denominations
came *teaching evolution* and a non-supernatural view of the Bible.
Methodist, Presbyterian, Congregational, and Northern Baptist schools
were especially hard hit. Bertrand Russell came from England preaching
atheism and socialism. Destructive books brought by such teachers
further undermined orthodox Christianity. **The Chinese intelligentsia
who had been schooled by orthodox evangelical missionaries were thus
softened for the advent of Marxism** (emphasis mine). Evolution is
destroying the church and society today, and Christians need to be
awakened to that fact."

Sowing and Reaping

Think about the parable of the sower of the seed (Matthew 13:3-

23). When the seed fell on rocky and thorny ground, it could not grow. It only grew when it fell on prepared ground. We throw the seed out: that represents the Gospel. It is falling on the thorny ground and rocky ground of evolutionary philosophy. The Gospel needs prepared ground. Creation evangelism enables us to prepare the ground so the good seed can be scattered and a great harvest reaped. Imagine what would happen if our churches really stood up for creation in our society! Creation evangelism is one of the means whereby we could see revival.

We are not suggesting that a true revival can be engineered by simply adopting certain clever human strategies. Revival is essentially the sovereign work of God pouring our His Spirit. But the history of the church suggests that God's movement in this area is related to the faithful prayer of His people and to the faithful preaching of the Gospel, giving due honor to God and His Word. Note the nature of the "everlasting Gospel" preached by the angel in Revelation 14:7 (NIV): "Fear God and give Him glory, because the hour of His judgment has come. Worship Him who made the heavens, the earth, the sea and the springs of water." Can the body of Christ really expect a great outpouring of God's Spirit in revival while we tolerate and compromise with a religious system (evolution) that was set up primarily to deny God the glory and worship due to Him as the great Creator, Judge and Redeemer?

As a result of the Creation Science ministry, many people who previously would not listen to the Gospel have realized that evolution is not proven scientific fact. They have heard the message of creation and redemption, and they have committed their lives to our Lord Jesus Christ. Large numbers of Christians have testified that their faith in the Scriptures has been restored. Instead of coming to the Bible with doubts, they know that it really is the Word of God. They can share the facts of Christianity with their neighbors and friends without wondering whether the Bible can be trusted. Christians have also had their eyes opened to the truth that to comprehend Christianity they have to understand the foundational book of Genesis.

After hearing me preach on this particular topic, a minister at one church informed his congregation that he had not realized before what he had been doing in his ministry in attempting to combat humanistic philosophy. He was, as it were, "cutting the tops off the weeds." The weeds kept growing back bigger and better than before. After listening to the message on creation evangelism, he realized this was simply not good enough. He had to remove the pestilence, roots and all. The creation ministry is a plowing ministry: plowing up the ground, getting rid of the barrier of evolution (getting rid of the weeds), and preparing the ground for the seed to be planted.

The following are excerpts from a few of the many thousands of letters that have come across my desk during my involvement with creation ministries. As you read these, notice the way in which people's lives have been affected by the message that this book details. The letters speak for themselves.

"I would like to simply say keep up the good work. I will never be able to thank you enough for bringing Creation Science to me. Since that day, I feel like you pulled a huge blind from in front of me." *Mr. G.*

"Thanks for your sound advice in encouraging a brother who I mentioned had made a stand after me as a result of the Creation Science seminar. I am now very pleased to say that I enjoy fellowship with another brother in the Lord as I have watched, in amazement, the consistent accelerating growth he has experienced over the months that have passed since your last visit. Seldom these days do we hear a message of such significance and relevance to the 20th century, where we are confronted with a society where most people haven't a clue as to where society came from and, as a result, haven't a clue where society is going. The modern philosophy appears to be 'let's live for today.' The whole problem being we don't want to learn from the past, the way men have lived and the results of their lifestyle because when we look at the past we see how fragile the whole of life is, showing the dependency on a God this generation appears to exclude." *Mr. P.*

"I would like you to know how exciting and beneficial it has been to read your material and listen to the tapes. It has so increased my faith in my God, through the understanding of His Bible, especially in the book of Genesis. I have just led a group of women in my church through a study of creation versus evolution, and have been really encouraged by the interest and response. I must confess I find it hard to be diplomatic, and not shout my new found knowledge from the roof tops!" *Mrs. L.*

"You may be encouraged to know that following the Creation Science Men's Breakfast held at the local church, my elderly neighbor became very interested in Christianity and after a few long chats, church services, and discussions, he became a Christian. He was baptized last year and is now an active seeking member of the church. His thirst to read the Scriptures puts me to shame, his face seems to glow now. He has been transformed totally!" *Mr. P.*

"I wish to share with you as part of my testimony. Almost a year ago I trusted in the Lord Jesus Christ as my personal Savior, partly as a result of the Creation Science ministry. As a consequence, the Lord had led me from the secular, evolutionary, humanistic state education system to a Christian school. My personal thanks to your ministry." *Mr. H.*

"As a former theistic evolutionist I now realize, thanks to the witness of Creation Science materials supporting the literal, historical accuracy of the Genesis record of Creation, that the evolution theory of origins is a false teaching." *Mr. D.*

"My son Brendan (eight years old) has made a commitment of his life to our Savior, Jesus. I realize that he does not fully understand the depth of what he has done, but the experience was very emotional for him, and he was sincere. May God guide me in training him further. I give thanks to your organization for the literature I have been able to purchase. This material from you increased my faith and I am sure it has been the inducement for my son's spiritual growth. I just can't thank you people enough." *Mr. N.*

"Thank you for sending me your publications. I described many of the discoveries in them and lent the material to my friend who is an electrical engineering student whom I tutor in mathematics. He, too, has found them very fascinating. This made him open to the Gospel, and he told me that he desired to read the Bible and other literature. I was only too happy to help. He intends to make his commitment to the Lord Jesus. All this happened through your publications." *Mr. J.*

"The time you spoke at the Baptist church on the relevance of creation —the message directed at Christians—there was a hardened atheist in the audience who had been prayed for and witnessed to for years. He came to the Lord that night after you left. God is really using this ministry." *Mr. W.*

"As a university lecturer in physiology, I was once an ardent evolutionist. I was in love with the theory and accepted it as fact, but not any more. Special creation is a belief, and likewise the theories of evolution are beliefs. These beliefs are about something that happened in the past; something that cannot be repeated, and therefore cannot be actually proven. As scientists seeking the truth, then, we are obliged to consider the evidence supporting each of the alternatives—to openly consider which model or belief best fits the observable facts.

"When I became a 'born again' Christian, a whole wonderful new life opened up for me. It was then that I began to question the theories of evolution, but I was not willing to change from evolutionist to creationist unless I could be convinced that scientific evidence justified that change.

"Literature presenting the scientific case for creation, as against evolution, is not widely available because of the general acceptance of evolution in our society. When I found that literature, however, I realized that evidence from all branches of science very clearly supports the Bible account of creation and a catastrophic, worldwide flood, rather than any of the theories of evolution. A growing number of eminently qualifed scientists in this and other countries are of this same opinion." *Dr. M.*

In addition to the many letters, I can also provide testimony to many incidents that have occurred as a result of creation speakers conducting programs throughout the world. A few of these incidents are listed below.

A young man informed us that he had brought five non-Christians to a seminar that the Creation Science Foundation had conducted. Two weeks later, they all committed their lives to the Lord! He informed us it was the Creation Science seminar that the Lord used to bring them to Himself.

At another church, a lady came and told us that she had bought materials we recommended at that church last year. After she took them home to her husband, who had never attended church, he had read the materials and had been attending church ever since.

In New Zealand a man approached us and said, "I have attended this church for 55 years and never heard a message anything like that." The message was the relevance of creation to understanding the Bible, the creation ordinances and the whole matter of the good earth, the Fall, and the necessity of the death of Jesus Christ for the salvation of mankind.

In the United States, similar responses to the creation ministries have been experienced over many years. The Institute for Creation Research also has had thousands of letters from people whose lives have been changed!

Creation evangelism is successful. So successful, in fact, that creation ministries are growing rapidly around the world. Ministries like the Institute for Creation Research in the United States and the Creation Science Foundation in Australia are not able to keep up with the work-load from the ever increasing demands for their services. *Lives are being changed.* People are coming to know the Lord Jesus Christ as Savior. The foundations of creation are being restored little by little. Are you, dear reader, a part of this growing, exciting and vital ministry in these last days?

We can only exclaim with the Psalmist in his words in Psalm 119 (KJV):

"Thy word have I hid in my heart, that I might not sin against Thee" (verse 11);

"Oh how love I Thy law! It is my meditation" (verse 97);

"I have more understanding than all my teachers: for Thy testimonies are my meditation" (verse 99);

"Through Thy precepts I get understanding: therefore I hate every false way" (verse 104);

"Thy word is a lantern unto my feet, and a light unto my path" (verse 105);

"The entrance of Thy words giveth light: it giveth understanding unto the simple" (verse 130);

"Thy word is very pure: therefore Thy servant loveth it" (verse 140);

"Thy law is the truth" (verse 142);

"Thy commandments are my delights" (verse 143);

"All Thy commandments are truth" (verse 151);

"Thy word is true from the beginning" (verse 160).

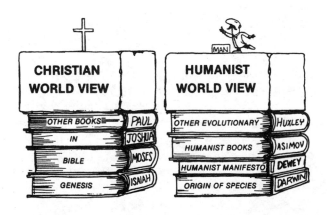

CHAPTER 10

Wake Up, Shepherds!

Much opposition to the creation ministry comes from within the church, particularly from those who have compromised with evolutionism and those who hold to liberal theology. First, please understand that I do not want to sound as if I am hitting too hard at those who have compromised between evolutionism and the Bible. Many people simply do not understand the real issues involved. They really believe scientists have proven evolution and every related issue. For many people, a belief in such positions as theistic evolution, the Gap Theory and progressive creation came out of sheer pressure from their belief that scientists had proved many, if not all, aspects of evolution. Until relatively recently, Christians had not conducted a great deal of scientific research to be able to explain all the problems with the theory of evolution. For many, holding to the aforementioned compromises gave some ability to cope with a confusing array of supposed "facts."

At one seminar, a lady told me that evolutionism had destroyed her faith in the Scriptures. She had such an emptiness in her life that she cried to the Lord and prayed for a solution to this problem. She was finding it impossible to trust the Scriptures. She was led to a library and happened to find a book on the Gap Theory. (The Gap Theory basically allows for billions of years between Genesis 1:1 and Genesis 1:2.) She was thrilled at this explanation and set about rebuilding her Christian life. At the end of the seminar, she came to me and exclaimed what a thrill it was now to know she did not have to believe the Gap Theory. She did say, though, that the Lord used the Gap Theory to bring her out of a situation that was caused by evolutionism.

Now she could totally trust the Bible.

There have been many great Christian men and women in past generations who promoted the Gap Theory or theistic evolution. However, now that we can show the real nature of evolutionist scientific research and can see the powerful evidence supporting the Bible in every area, there is no need to cling to these positions of compromise. Not only is there no need, but it is imperative that Christians give up these positions and accept the Bible as the authoritative Word of God.

James 3:1 (NIV) warns us: "Not many of you should presume to be teachers, my brothers, because you know that we who teach will be judged more strictly."

I am appealing to all Christian leaders to consider seriously their beliefs about the question of creation/evolution. One example, which I quoted earlier, described a visit to a school and the resultant openness of the students to the Gospel message. I shared the testimony of a young student from that school. One of the things I did not mention was the virulent opposition of two ministers from that district who tried to bar my entrance to the school. Their reason? They said I would only confuse the students. They indicated that I had no right to insist that the Bible be taken literally. If they had been successful in their endeavor, many of those students would not now be open to the Gospel.

At another school one of the local ministers spent a great deal of time obtaining special permission for the Creation Science team to speak to some of the classes. Another local minister went to the school and demanded the right to speak after we had spoken. He told the students that he was a Christian and a minister of religion, and then appealed to them not to believe what we were saying. He said he believed in evolution and did not believe Genesis was true.

Such events have occurred many times during my experience as a creation ministries' speaker. Again and again, we hear ministers claim that we would only confuse students and so should not be allowed into schools. These ministers are oblivious to the fact that students are being told there is no God and everything (including man) is a result of random chance. Our message is simple. We are telling the students there is a God, that He is Creator, and the Bible can be trusted. How can men, who are supposed to be caring pastors, rather the students be told there is no God? These men have no faith in their own pilgrimage. How can they ever hope to shepherd others? They should actually visit the schools and ask the students what the teaching of evolutionism is doing to them.

In one church school in Tasmania, Australia, the official position was to teach evolution with God added to it. The local bishop tried his hardest to prevent my visit to the school, but one of the teachers was allowed to present the creationist position to the class, and he invited me as a special speaker. At the conclusion of my presentation, 69 of the 70 girls surrounded me and verbally attacked my stand on creation. They shouted statements such as: "There is no God!" "Buddhism is better than Christianity!" "Evolution is true!" "You can't trust the Bible!" "The Bible is full of mistakes!" "We are not interested in what you have to say." Because of the compromise with evolutionism, they were even less open to God's Word than public school students. They attended a "church" school. Why wouldn't they know the "truth?" So far as they were concerned, they already had all the answers. One young girl, however, came to me with tears in her eyes. She thanked me for the foundation given her faith. She said she was a Bible-believing Christian and that she found it very hard to be in that particular school, as the teachers were attempting to destroy her faith in Christianity. They had obviously weakened the faith of many of the other girls in the class.

During a question time at one church, the minister raised a vital question. Because there was no Christian school in the district that taught from the creationist perspective, should parents be advised to send their children to the local public school with its known anti-Christian philosophy or to the compromising Christian school? There was silence as the congregation awaited my answer.

What was my answer? Send their children to a church school which compromised with evolution and only taught a secular philosophy or to the local public school? My first answer was, "I would send them to neither—I would keep them home!" Of course, this is becoming a real option for many parents today, and the home school movement is growing. However, I did go on to add that it was easier in one sense to tell the students they were being taught an anti-Christian philosophy in the public school. A church school that is supposedly Christian but has compromised with secular philosophy is no different from the public schools, except that it purports to be Christian.

The Lord makes this clear to us in Revelation 3:15-16 (KJV). In reference to the compromising church, we read: "I know thy works, that thou art neither cold nor hot: I would thou wert cold or hot. So then because thou art then lukewarm, and neither cold nor hot, I will spew thee out of my mouth."

This is probably the reason why we often get a far better response to our ministry in public schools than in compromising Christian schools.

Pastors! Theologians! Ministers! You must be aware of what evolution is doing to students' minds. You must be aware of what is happening in the school system. There are fewer children attending our church education programs. There are fewer children interested in religious education in schools. In many schools, religious education classes are not allowed any more. Look at it practically. Is your compromised position working? It is not!

Some of the opposition we encounter could be seen in the interview on Australian radio on May 16, 1984, with the Rev. Colin Honey, a Uniting Church minister and Master of Kingswood College at the University of Western Australia. The Rev. Honey was asked if he saw a fundamental confusion between Christianity and simplemindedness. He replied, "I guess there will be in people's minds if fools keep telling us that the Bible says the world was created in six days."

You would be in for a shock if you wrote to some of our theological or Bible colleges and asked them what they teach in that college about creation. But be very specific—don't just ask them if they teach creation. Ask them what they believe about Genesis. Do they believe the days were real days? Do they believe the Flood of Noah was world-wide in extent? Do they take Genesis literally? Do they see the importance of Genesis to doctrine? I have often said to people in churches that I knew the theological college of that particular denomination either taught evolution or the view that Genesis does not matter. Most people reel in shock. They had believed their theological colleges taught that the Bible is true. **One of the problems we have in the West is that most theological and Bible colleges produce ministers who have been trained to question the Scriptures rather than accept them. That is why we have so many shepherds in our churches who are really leading the sheep astray.** If you support any of these institutions financially, why not ask them what they teach about these matters?

At one seminar three ministers from a Protestant denomination came up to me. They said that what I was teaching was a perversion of the Scriptures. As we talked, it became obvious that we were arguing from two totally different approaches to the Scripture. I asked these people how God made the first woman. I said the Bible claims that God took from Adam's side and made a woman—did they believe that? Their answer went something like this: "Yes, we do believe the symbolic picture implied here that men and women are one." "No," I said, "I asked you whether you believed that that is how God actually made a woman." They said they certainly agreed that this theological picture implied that men and women are one. I repeated my question a number of times, saying that the Bible claims this is actually how God made a woman. Not only that, but in the New Testament in I Corinthians 11:8, we read where Paul states that the woman came from the man and not the man from the woman, obviously supporting the historical creation account in Genesis.

We were getting nowhere, so I asked them if they believed that Jesus was nailed on a cross as the New Testament states. "Oh, yes," they said, "we certainly believe that." I then asked them why they did not believe God actually took Adam's side and made a woman. They told me it was the difference between accepting Genesis as poetry rather than history, suggesting that if it were poetry it should not be believed.

Genesis, of course, is history. And, besides, even if something is written in poetic form, as indeed other parts of the Scriptures are, does this then say that we do not believe it?

They informed me that, for much of Scripture, it was not what was said that was important, but the theological picture that was implied. I asked them how they determined what that theological picture was, on what basis did they decide what was the true theological picture, and how could they be sure that their approach to Scripture was the right one? From where did they obtain their authority to approach the Scripture this way? They said it was their study of history and theology over the years that enabled them to decide what was the correct way to approach Scripture and to determine what these symbolic pictures were. I then told them it sounded as though they simply held an opinion as to how to approach Scripture. How did they know it was the right opinion? This is where the conversation abruptly ended. These men want to tell God what He is saying rather than letting God tell them what the truth is. This is the position of many theological leaders.

After speaking at a church in Victoria, Australia, one of the local ministers (who was obviously upset) told me in front of a large number of people that I had no right to force my interpretation of the Bible on others. He was extremely vocal and emotional about this issue. The thing I found amazing was that he was trying to enforce his interpretation of the Bible on me and the others that were present. He could not comprehend that aspect.

There are many passages throughout the Bible in which God rebukes religious leaders for leading people astray. Jeremiah, for instance, was called by the Lord to warn the Israelites about teachers and priests who were not proclaiming the truth. Jesus openly rebuked many religious leaders, calling them such names as "vipers" (Matthew 12:34).

These same warnings apply to many today who claim to be teachers of the Word of God, but who, in reality, are causing many people to fall by the wayside. Many of you will no doubt be aware that much of the opposition to the work of the creation organizations worldwide comes from theologians and other religious leaders. Many of the humanist groups often enlist people who claim to be Christians but believe in evolution to support them on television, radio, and in publications in their effort to combat the creation ministries. I have seen TV reporters and radio announcers revelling in the fact that they can have someone on their program who claims to be a Christian but opposes the Bible and creation.

At one creation-versus-evolution debate, an evolutionist stated that the issue was not whether God created or not. He said that he believed in creation and that he was a Christian. He then went on to vehemently attack the Bible and Christianity. During the question time, someone in the audience asked this person whether he could testify to Jesus Christ being his personal Savior. The evolutionist debater, caught off-guard, was obviously wanting to avoid the question. However, he decided to attempt an answer. He told the audience he did not use the same terminology as others, and that he certainly did not accept the Bible at all and would not have anything to do with fundamental Christianity. Basically, he described fundamental Christianity as the belief that accepted the Bible as true. Yet, many probably had believed that he was a Christian because he publicly stated so. Here was a wolf in sheep's clothing leading sheep astray.

Many shepherds of the sheep in today's world can be found in one of the following groups, in the sliding progression from "toleration" to "capitulation to error."

1. Toleration

Many tell us we should tolerate other people's beliefs about evolution: that we must refrain from speaking against what they say. Or, we are told to consider all the alternatives that scientists put before us and not be "dogmatic" about one view. Of course, this is a form of dogmatism itself, claiming that we cannot insist Genesis be taken literally so as to exclude evolutionary philosophy. Many theological colleges dogmatically insist that students consider all views on the interpretation of Genesis (e.g., theistic evolution, progressive creation, Day-Age Theory, Gap Theory, Six-Day Literal Creation), and go on to assert that no one person may say that any view is definitely correct, or incorrect! I am not suggesting that students at such colleges should not be made aware of these other positions, however, the fallacies of these positions should be pointed out in detail.

2. Accommodation

Many are saying that you cannot be sure what Genesis means or says, and perhaps the evolutionists are right after all. Because of the high respect for "academia," and the immense amount of material from a large number of scientists pushing evolution, many Christians just add evolution to the Bible.

3. Cooperation

Here the error of evolution has been tolerated and given standing in the church. This has become a comfortable position because there is great harmony: the people in the church who believe in evolution don't feel threatened, and they can all work together. Such people claim that God created, but if He worked through evolution, it does not really matter.

4. Contamination

With people becoming so intimately involved with the error of evolutionary philosophy, this theory becomes generally accepted and taught through the churches, Sunday schools, Christian schools and religious educational programs as well as in the secular school classrooms. Consequently, the issue doesn't bother people any more.

5. Capitulation to Error

Evolution becomes accepted as fact, and anyone who dares to disagree is a "heretic." As people accept evolution, and relegate Genesis to myth or allegory, they start to question the rest of Scripture. A rejection of the foundations of all doctrine contained in the book of Genesis logically leads one to a denial of the entire Bible. Liberal theology becomes rampant.

It was interesting to note the reaction of a professor in Genetics and Human Variation at the School of Biological Sciences at LaTrobe University. When he was asked a question during a debate with Dr. Gary Parker relating to the fact that many Christians do accept evolution, he stated: "I can only add that Christianity is fairly widely fragmented. Obviously, Christianity is in various stages of evolution; some sections of it seem to have just about dispensed with the theology altogether. It seems to be that the ultimate stage of evolution of Christianity will just be to throw out all the theology and be left with an entirely rational and naturalistic system of outlook on life." What he recognized, of course, was that there is really no difference between atheistic and theistic evolution—except that in the latter God is added to the system. Logically, therefore, theistic evolution is only one step away from atheistic evolution, and that is where he sees the ultimate end of such a compromise situation.

In many denominations, there is real controversy and a lot of discussion concerning inerrrancy of the Bible. When discussing this issue, the sad thing is that many evangelical scholars do not recognize or deliberately sidestep the importance of Genesis. The acceptance of the literal events in Genesis is foundational to the question of Biblical inerrancy. If the conferences on inerrancy were to settle that issue first, the rest of the problems they have would disappear very quickly. This is another reason why any Statement of Faith being formulated for Christian schools, Christian organizations, churches and such conferences should always be very specific concerning Genesis. It is not good enough to say that they believe God created. They need to understand the importance and relevance of accepting Genesis literally, of rejecting evolution completely, and of understanding the foundational nature of Genesis to the rest of the Bible.

Unfortunately, even much of the Christian school movement is devoid of this understanding. I know of Christian schools that are more concerned with their teacher's view of eschatology (the second coming) than with what they believe and understand concerning the foundational issue of creation. This means they do not fully understand Christian education!

As the prophet Hosea says (4:14, NIV), "a people without understanding will come to ruin!" While there are many shepherds leading the sheep astray, we must remember that the sheep are also to blame, as God tells us through Jeremiah 5:31 (NIV): "The prophets prophesy lies, the priests rule by their own authority, and *my people love it this way . . .*" (emphasis mine). Let us pray that more men and women in our nations will be prepared to stand for the absolute truth of God's Holy Word.

Exodus 20:11 (KJV) states: "For in six days the Lord made the heavens and the earth, the sea, and all that is in them, and rested the seventh day. Therefore, the Lord blessed the Sabbath day and hallowed it."

A child in a Christian school class asked her teacher, "How could anybody create everything in six days from nothing?" Another very discerning young student blurted out, "But God is just not *anybody!*"

ALL SCRIPTURE IS INSPIRED BY GOD

THIS SCRIPTURE INSCRIBED BY GOD
EXODUS 20:11

CHAPTER 11

Creation, Flood and Coming Fire

There is a prophecy in II Peter 3 concerning the last days of this earth's history, and it very much relates to the whole creation/evolution issue.

II Peter 3:3-7 (NIV) states: "First of all, you must understand that in the last days scoffers will come, scoffing and following their own evil desires. They will say, 'Where is this coming He promised? Ever since our fathers died, everything goes on as it has since the beginning of creation.' But they deliberately forget that long ago by God's Word the heavens existed and the earth was formed out of water with water. By water also the world of that time was deluged and destroyed. By the same word the present heavens and earth are reserved for fire, being kept for the day of judgment and destruction of ungodly men."

"ALL THINGS CONTINUE . . . "

Notice that the Scriptures are warning us that in the last days people are going to be saying "everything goes on as it has since the beginning of creation." Evolutionists tell us that the earth has been in existence for millions of years and that life started evolving on this earth millions of years ago. Many Christians also hold this same belief. Geologists have the idea the the processes we see operating in the present world have been going on for millions of years at essentially the same rate, and will probably go on for millions of years into the future as well.

The technical word used in geology for this belief is "uniformitarianism." For example, the desert museum in Tucson, Arizona, not only has a display for people to see what supposedly has happened over the past millions of years, but it also has a display of what many scientists believe will happen to Arizona over the millions of years they believe are to come!

Evolutionists, atheistic and theistic, use the phrase "the present is the key to the past." In other words, they say that the way to understand the past is to observe what happens in the present. For instance, they say that since fossils form rarely in today's world, the vast layers of rock containing billions of fossils over most of the earth's surface must have taken millions of years. Evolutionists tell us that since we observe mutations (that is, accidental changes in our genes) occurring today, these must have occurred ever since the dawn of time. Thus, mutations must be one of the mechanisms involved in the postulated evolutionary progression. The Bible, on the other hand, tells us that there was a time when there was no sin, and thus there was neither animal nor human death, nor disease, nor mistakes. Mutations are **mistakes** that occur in our genes, and they are virtually all harmful. Those who believe in evolution have to assume that evolution is occurring today to be able to say that what we see today are the same processes that have gone on for millions of years. Thus, to be consistent, the Christian who believes in evolution should also believe that man is still evolving today.

How can we establish beyond doubt the details of an event that supposedly happened in the past? One way is to find witnesses who were there, or look for records written by witnesses. Therefore, the only way we can ever know for sure exactly what happened in the geological past is if there was someone who was there at the time (a witness) who could tell us whether geological processes have always been the same or whether at some time geological processes have been different. The Bible claims to be the record of One (God) who not only knows everything, but who has always been there because He is outside of time. In fact, He created time. The Bible claims that God moved men through His Spirit to write down His words, and that they are not just the words of men but the Word of God (I Thessalonians 2:13, II Peter 1:20-21). The book of Genesis claims to be the record from God telling us of the events of creation and of other events in this world's early history which have great bearing upon our present circumstances. Thus, the present is not the key to the past. Rather, revelation is the key to the past.

The revelation in Genesis tells us about such events as creation, Noah's Flood and the Tower of Babel. These are events that have made the earth's geology, geography, biology, etc., what they are today. Therefore, we must also realize that what happened in the past is the key to the present. The entrance of sin into the world explains why we have death and why we have mistakes occurring in our genes. The global devastation caused by Noah's Flood helps to explain the fossil record. The events at the Tower of Babel help us to come to an understanding of the origin of the different nations and cultures around the world.

Today evolutionists deny that the Biblical record can be taken seriously. They put their faith in their belief that "all things continue as they have done from the beginning . . . ." The prophecy in II Peter 3 is being fulfilled before our very eyes.

"WILLINGLY IGNORANT . . . "

In the next section of this prophecy we are told that men will deliberately reject three things. Notice that the emphasis here is on a deliberate rejection, or as some translations put it, a "willing ignorance." Thus, it is a deliberate action on a person's part not to believe:

(a) God created the world, which at first was covered with water (which means that its surface was cool at the beginning, not a molten blob as evolutionists teach).

(b) God once judged this world with a global, cataclysmic flood at the time of Noah.

(c) God is going to judge this world again, but the next time it will be by fire.

People often make the statement: "If there is so much evidence that God created the world and sent a global cataclysmic flood, then surely all scientists would believe this." The solution is given here in II Peter 3. It is not simply a matter of providing evidence to convince people, for people do not want to be convinced. We read in Romans 1:20 that there is enough evidence to convince everyone that God is Creator, so much so that we are condemned if we do not believe. Furthermore,

Romans 1:18 tells us that men "suppress the truth in unrighteousness." It is not a matter of lack of evidence to convince people that the Bible is true; the problem is that they do not **want** to believe the Bible. The reason for this is obvious. If people believed in the God of the Bible, they would have to acknowledge His authority and obey the rules He has laid down. However, every human being suffers from the same problem—the sin which Adam committed in the Garden of Eden—a "disease" which we all inherit. Adam's sin was rebellion against God's authority. Likewise, people everywhere today are in rebellion against God, so to admit that the Bible is true would be an admission of their own sinful and rebellious nature and of their need to be born again by cleansing through the blood of Christ.

It is easy to see this "willing ignorance" in action when watching debates over the creation/evolution issue. In most cases, the evolutionists are not interested in the wealth of data, evidence and information the creationists put forward. They usually try to attack creationists by attempting to destroy their credibility. They are not interested in data, logical reasoning, or any evidence that points to creation or refutes evolution, because they are totally committed to their religious faith called evolution.

Modern geology today tells us that there never was a world-wide flood as described in the Bible. We are told that millions of years of geological processes can explain the enormous fossil record in the sedimentary rock layers around the earth's surface. However, creationists have shown that the fossil-bearing rock layers were produced by enormous catastrophic processes consistent with Noah's Flood.[1] But evolutionists refuse to accept this, for to do so would mean that the Bible is right, and thus the whole of their evolutionary philosophy would have to be rejected. These people are "willingly ignorant" about

---

[1] In recent years, partly because of the success of creationist geologists in pointing out the clear evidence of rapid processes in the rocks, many evolutionary geologists have begun to abandon the "slow and gradual" view in favor of the idea that there were many great catastrophes in the earth's history responsible for shaping it. However, their opposition to the catastrophe described in the Bible is as vehement and as "willfully ignorant" as ever. A more complete treatment of this area can be found in the literature mentioned in the list of resources at the end of this book.

the facts that do not support their evolutionary ideas but do fit into a model of geology based upon what the Bible says concerning Noah's Flood. This is another fulfillment of prophecy before our very eyes.

Much of the scientific literature also tells us that most scientists expect this world to go on and on for millions of years. The example of the desert museum in Tucson, Arizona, is again appropriate. As mentioned before, one display at this museum is supposed to represent what scientists believe will happen in Arizona over the next few millions of years or so. People often look at that display and ask the question: "How can they know what is going to happen millions of years into the future?" The answer is: "In exactly the same way they understand what has happened millions of years in the past!" They do not know—it is only their guess. If scientists agreed that God had created, that Noah's Flood was a real event and that, therefore, the Bible was true, they would have to tell quite a different story. Since Jesus Christ in Matthew 24:37-39 uses the event of Noah's Flood as a warning that God has judged the earth, and will judge it again, they would have to agree that God is going to come back as Judge. The next time He will use fire as the method of judgment rather than water. Sinful man in rebellion against God does not want to admit that he must stand before the God of creation one day and account for his life. Thus, in rejecting creation and Noah's Flood, and claiming "scientific" evidence that supposedly supports his own belief, he becomes comfortable in not thinking about the coming judgment. But, just as God created the world by His Word and sent the Flood through His Word, so God will judge this world by fire.

CONCLUSION

The earth, sun, moon, and stars stand as memorials to the fact that God has created. The fossil record is an immense memorial to the fact that God has judged by water. All of this should warn each man, woman and child that, just as God has kept His Word in the past concerning judgment, so He will keep His Word in the future concerning judgment.

II Peter 3 contains a prophecy concerning the last days: a prophecy we are seeing fulfilled before our very eyes. Let us, therefore, become more vigorous and bold in witnessing for our God, the God of creation.

THE GOSPEL

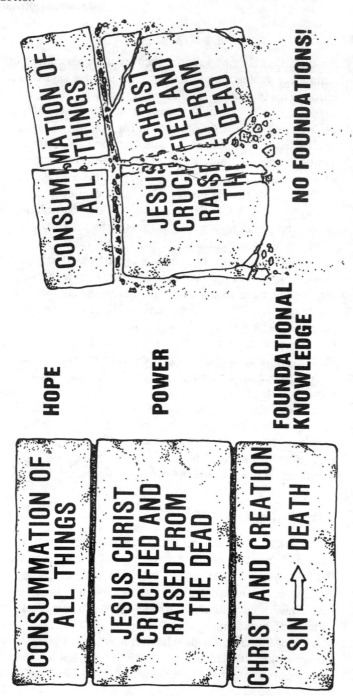

HOPE

CONSUMMATION OF ALL THINGS

POWER

JESUS CHRIST CRUCIFIED AND RAISED FROM THE DEAD

FOUNDATIONAL KNOWLEDGE

CHRIST AND CREATION

SIN ⟹ DEATH

NO FOUNDATIONS!

"Since everything will be destroyed in this way, what kind of people ought you to be? You ought to live holy and godly lives as you look forward to the day of God and speed its coming" (II Peter 3:11-12a, NIV).

Isaac Asimov, an active anti-creationist, has given warnings about creationists. He has been quoted as saying (in regard to creationists getting equal time for presenting the creation model in schools), it is "today equal time, tomorrow the world." Isaac Asimov is right! We are out to convince the world that Jesus Christ is Creator. Isaac Asimov is one who has signed the *Humanist Manifesto*—he is out to convince the world that Jesus Christ is not the Creator.

We are out to convince people like Isaac Asimov that Jesus Christ is Creator. Why? Because we want a good fight? Because we like controversy? No, because we know that those who do not trust the Lord will spend eternity separated from Him. And what happens to those of us who do accept the salvation offered by Christ? "They will be His people, and God Himself will be with them and be their God. He will wipe every tear from their eyes. There will be **no more death or mourning or crying or pain,** for the old order of things has passed away" (Revelation 21:3b-4, NIV).

RESOURCES

The following list of resources is recommended for researching further into the topics referred to in this book.

All books can be obtained in the United States through Master Books, and in Australia through Creation Science Foundation, Ltd. Addresses are given in section 18 below.

1. **A Is for Adam** — Ken and Mally Ham (Master Books, Green Forest, AR, 1995). This is a children's rhyme book with notes designed to give you background information for each rhyme, thus equipping you to explain the concepts in greater detail. It is like reading a commentary on the Book of Genesis!

2. **Answers Book, The** — Ken Ham, Dr. Andrew Snelling, and Dr. Carl Wieland (Master Books, Green Forest, AR, 1992). Now you can have at your fingertips solid answers to those puzzling questions on creation/evolution and the Bible that are so often avoided or sidestepped, even though they come up all the time. How did the kangaroo get to Australia? Where did Cain get his wife? Dinosaurs? Where did all the races come from? Were there ice ages? Carbon-dating? Drifting continents? Fangs in Eden? Noah's flood: Where did all the water go? What about the gap theory? Star-time? Six-day creation? Detailed answers to the 12 most-asked questions on creation and evolution. Plus: each answer includes a brief summary to help you grasp the idea at a glance.

3. **Bone of Contention** — Sylvia Baker, Creation Science Foundation Ltd., Australia for Evangelical Press, England, Second Impression, 1987. This is one of the best brief overviews of the

whole creation/evolution question. Thousands of copies have been distributed around the world, and many people give testimony that they became Christians as a result of this particular book.

4. **Bones of Contention** — Marvin L. Lubenow (Baker Books, Grand Rapids, MI, 1992). One of the best and most recent publications available that documents the intriguing background and information about the various so-called ape-men. After reading this book you will be shocked to find how brainwashed we have been about this issue. A thoroughly researched work that details information on all the familiar ape-men we were taught about in school: Neanderthan Man, Nebraska Man, Piltdown Man, Peking Man, etc. Great chapters that help Christians understand why evolution cannot be accepted, and an intriguing section on who wrote Genesis.

5. *Creation* magazine — published quarterly by the Creation Science Foundation Ltd., Australia, and is distributed in the United States by Answers in Genesis, Florence, Kentucky. This magazine is produced in glossy style with many full-color photos and illustrations. Each issue covers various aspects of creation/evolution and related topics. This can be used very effectively in witnessing as well as in educating the whole family. Yearly subscriptions are available, and back issues may be purchased if available.

6. **Creation: Facts of Life** — Dr. Gary Parker (Master Books, Green Forest, AR, 1994). A leading creation scientist and speaker presents the classic arguments for evolution used in public schools, universities, and the media, and refutes them in an entertaining and easy-to-read style. Once an evolutionist, Dr. Parker is well qualified to refute these arguments. A must for students and teachers alike.

7. **Genesis Record, The** — Henry M. Morris (Baker Book House, Grand Rapids, MI, 1976). A verse by verse commentary through the entire Book of Genesis. Dr. Henry Morris, in an easy-to-

understand style, explains all the biblical and scientific aspects of creation. As all Christian doctrine ultimately has its basis in the Book of Genesis, it is absolutely vital that every Christian believe and understand this book in order to understand what Christianity is all about. This is a scientific devotional in narrative style — the "Rolls Royce" of creation books!

8. **In the Minds of Men** — Ian T. Taylor (TFE Publishing, Toronto, Canada, 1984). The best layman's summary on all of the historical aspects of the evolutionary philosophy and its effect on men's thinking.

9. **Life Before Birth** — Dr. Gary Parker (Master Books, Green Forest, AR, 1992). Were we people before we were born? Do we have useless leftover animal parts inside us? Dr. Gary Parker's popular Christian family book, reprinted and revised in a colorful format, brilliantly combines a family teaching book about development of a human being from the DNA upwards (and tasteful sex education), with a very powerful pro-life, pro-creation, pro-family, and pro-Christian message. Highly recommended for every Christian family.

10. **The Long War Against God** — Dr. Henry M. Morris (Baker Book House, Grand Rapids, MI, 1992). Another of Dr. Morris' classic works which deals with the relevance of creation to the Christian. Dr. Morris, in this thoroughly researched masterpiece, documents the history of the creation/evolution conflict and its effect on nations down through the ages. Very rich! Your understanding of the creation/evolution issue will never be the same after reading this work. Contains over 500 quotes and citations. (Semi-technical)

11. **Starlight and Time** — Dr. D. Russell Humphreys (Master Books, Green Forest, AR, 1994). The Bible teaches the universe is just thousands of years old and yet we can see stars that are billions of light-years away. In his book Dr. Humphreys explains his new cosmology with an easy-to-read popular summary and has included two technical papers.

12. **Stones and Bones** — Dr. Carl Wieland (Master Books, Green Forest, AR, 1994). Basic reasons why Christians (and some non-Christians) reject evolution in favor of creation. Easy-to-understand explanations on fossils, missing links, mutations, dinosaurs, natural selection, and more.

13. **Understanding the Times** — David A. Noebel (Summit Press, Manitou Springs, CO, 1991). Most Christians don't fully understand the world we live in. What are today's dominant worldviews? How can they be refuted? Extremely well-documented and indexed.

14. **The Young Earth** — Dr. John D. Morris (Master Books, Green Forest, AR, 1994). The book we've all been waiting for! Dr. John Morris, a geologist, explains in easy-to-understand terms how true science supports a young earth. Filled with facts that will equip laymen and scientists alike.

15. **Video Series — Answers in Genesis** — Ken Ham and Dr. Gary Parker. These 12 videos cover an entire AIG seminar. They feature everything from Dr. Gary Parker's testimony of how he changed from an evolutionist to a creationist, and includes Ken' challenging message on creation evangelism. Available from Master Books.

16. **Creation newsletters** — Newsletters are available from the following organizations free on request. These newsletters usually detail the activities of the corresponding organization, as well as include important teaching on many aspects of the creation/evolution controversy.

    (a) **Answers in Genesis**, published monthly by Answers in Genesis, P.O. Box 6330, Florence, KY 41022-6330, USA; phone (606) 727-2222.

    (b) **Creation Science Prayer News**, published quarterly by Creation Science Foundation Ltd., P.O. Box 6302, Acacia Ridge DC, Qld 4110, Australia; phone (07) 3273-7650.

17. **Personnel Available for Ministry** — Speakers gifted and trained in presenting biblical and/or scientific aspects of the creation/evolution controversy — from layman through to technical level — are available for teaching, preaching, debates, etc. In the United States contact Answers in Genesis, P.O. Box 6330, Florence KY 41022-6330; phone (606) 727-2222. In Australia contact the Creation Science Foundation, P.O. Box 6302, Acacia Ridge DC, Qld 4110, Australia; phone (07) 3273 7650.

18. **Other Books and Resources** — For a comprehensive listing of books and other resources available on the creation/evolution issue, write or phone the following organizations:

Master Books
P.O. Box 727
Green Forest, AR 72638
Phone: 1-800-999-3777
Fax: (870) 438-5120

Answers in Genesis
P.O. Box 6330
Florence, KY 41022-6330 USA
Phone: (606) 727-2222
Fax: (606) 727-2299

Creation Science Foundation Limited
P.O. Box 6302
Acacia Ridge DC, Qld 4110
Australia
Phone: (07) 3273 7650
Fax: (07) 3273 7672

Creation Science Foundation (UK)
P.O. Box 1427
Sevenhampton, Swindon, Wilts.,
SN6 7 UF, United Kingdom
Phone: (01 793) 512 268
Fax: (01 793) 861-1462

Creation Science Foundation (NZ)
215 Bleakhouse Road
Howick, Auckland, New Zealand
Phone: (09) 534-8914

Institute for Creation Research
P.O. Box 2667
El Cajon, CA 92021
Phone: (619) 448-0900
Fax: (619) 448-3469

APPENDIX 1

TWENTY REASONS WHY GENESIS AND EVOLUTION DO NOT MIX

Many people believe that they can add evolution to the Bible. They think that by doing this they can explain life coming about as a result of God's use of evolutionary processes. This position is known as "theistic evolution."[1] However, this is totally inconsistent with Scripture.

1. NO DEATH BEFORE ADAM'S FALL

Evolution teaches that for millions of years before man things have lived and died. They have fought and struggled, killed and been killed. It was a world without mercy—"nature red in tooth and claw." This history of evolution is a history of death. Death has been "from the beginning."

The Bible clearly teaches that death, particularly the physical and

---

[1]An offshoot of theistic evolution, which is sometimes promoted by Christians who are sensitive to criticism of evolution, is known as progressive creation. This idea holds that while life was developing through the vast ages imagined by evolutionists God stepped in at various times along the way. At each point He created something new which the evolutionary process could not accomplish without this help from God. Progressive creation implies that God's forethought in creation was not adequate for the complete evolutionary process at the beginning. It will be seen that the arguments against progressive creation are covered by the arguments against theistic evolution, particularly with reference to death and struggle existing before man.

spiritual death of man, entered the world only after the first man Adam sinned.

In Romans 5:12 (NIV) the Apostle Paul wrote: "Therefore, just as sin entered the world through one man, and death through sin, and in this way death came to all men, because all sinned." In I Corinthians 15:21-22 (NIV), "For since death came through a man, the resurrection of the dead comes also through a man. For as in Adam all die, so in Christ all will be made alive." In Genesis 3:22-23 (NIV) we read: "And the Lord God said, 'The man has now become like one of us, knowing good and evil. He must not be allowed to reach out his hand and take also from the Tree of Life and eat, and live for ever.' So the Lord God banished him from the Garden of Eden to work the ground from which he had been taken." Adam was sent out of the garden so he would not live for ever. In other words, he would have to die.

But what about the animals? Was death a part of the created animal world? There are a number of reasons why I believe animal death as well as human death did not occur before the Fall.

(a) **Could animals have died from old age?** Before the Fall animals could not have died of old age because Romans 8 reminds us that corruption and decay entered the world only with sin. Death by old age would have meant that animal bodies would have been wearing out and corruption would have existed. This would not fit with the description that before sin everything in God's creation was "good." Isaiah 51:6 (NIV) tells us that after sin "the earth will wear out like a garment . . . ." In Romans 8:22 (NIV) we read that because of sin "the whole creation has been groaning as in the pains of childbirth right up to the present time." Thus, it is obvious that the **whole** of creation, which must include all living creatures, has been subject to "the bondage of corruption" (Romans 8:21, KJV) only as a result of the curse because of Adam's sin. Death from old age, therefore, only began with the curse.

As we live in a world where everything wears out, it is difficult to understand how aging could not happen in the pre-Fall world. However, we are shown a glimpse of the solution in Deuteronomy 8:4 (NIV). God reminded the Israelites that during their wanderings in the wilderness their "clothes did not wear out" upon them, "and [their] feet did not swell during these forty years." Clearly, this was an unusual, supernatural preservation provided by God for His people's particular circumstances.

We do not see this happening today. Our clothes wear out quickly. However, when God sustains something totally, this wearing-out does not happen. It is obvious that before the Fall everything had been created "good," and nothing would have worn out.

(b) **Could animals have died when Adam, or other animals ate them for food?** Again, the answer would be "No!" Not only animals, but man and woman were told they were to eat only plants (Genesis 1:29).

Animals could not have died from eating each other; Genesis 1:30 tells us their food was also to be only plants. Also, as God created everything "good," animals could not have killed each other for the sake of killing. This would be opposite in meaning to "good." God, being a good God, would not create animals so that the stronger tried to eliminate the weak in a fight for survival. Also, as everything was created good, there could not have been disease to kill off animals or man. Diseases today contribute to our bodies' wearing out, but this would not be consistent with what has been pointed out earlier.

(c) **Could animals have died accidentally?** Again, this would go against the concept of "good." Such a question overlooks the sovereignty and greatness of God. As we have seen, God can sustain things so that even clothes don't wear out. Before sin came into the world, death wasn't even a question—God had total control of the creation and sustained it 100 percent! There was no corruption and no decay. Hence, death wasn't even a possibility. Adam was made in the image of the all-caring God, and the animals were in his charge. He cared for them. Death and bloodshed came into the world as a judgment from God for man's rebellion. But at the same time death was the very means by which man was to be redeemed. So bloodshed could not have existed before man's fall.

There was no bloodshed before Adam sinned: everything was perfect and death was not a part of animal existence. However, Adam did sin; and God, in giving His covenant to Adam, had laid down the condition that death was to be the reward of disobedience. We then read that God Himself was the first shedder of blood, because He gave Adam and Eve coats of skin to cover their nakedness (Genesis 3:21). There is no specific command recorded, but we do know that "Abel brought fat portions from some of the firstborn of his flock.

The Lord looked with favor on Abel and his offering" (Genesis 4:4, NIV). It is evident, then, that the requirement was understood. The writer of Hebrews (9:22, NIV) observes that "without the shedding of blood there is no forgiveness." God fulfilled two undertakings after the Fall: (a) that man should die as the penalty for his sin; and (b) that the Seed of the woman should bruise the serpent's head, and the serpent should bruise His heel. So death and bloodshed are the consequences of sin; the penalty which Christ, the last Adam, bore by His death and shedding of blood on the cross but triumphed over in His glorious resurrection for the redemption of man. If death and bloodshed existed before man sinned, the redemption message is nonsense.

Evolution teaches that death and bloodshed existed virtually from the beginning. Millions of years of animals fighting for survival—shedding blood and eating each other—is part of the mechanisms of evolution which brought man into existence. It is completely contrary to the Biblical history of the world.

Evolution says death plus struggle brought man into existence; the Bible says man's actions led to sin, which led to death. These two are totally contradictory. If evolution is true, then the reason Christ died on the cross has been destroyed.

2. ADAM DID NOT FALL "UPWARDS"

Christians talk about the fact that Adam "fell." The "Fall of Adam" refers to the fact that when God made everything it was perfect. However, because of his action, Adam was responsible for something terrible happening to the whole of creation. Romans 8:22 (NIV) says, "We know that the whole creation has been groaning as in the pains of childbirth right up to the present time." Because of Adam's sin, God cursed the whole of creation, including the stars, the ants, the elephants and people.

In Genesis we read, "So the Lord God said to the serpent, 'Because you have done this, cursed are you above all livestock'" (3:14, NIV). "Cursed is the ground because of you" (3:17, NIV). God placed a curse on the world because of Adam's rebellion. Therefore, the creation went from a perfect state to a cursed state. As a result of the curse, the whole of creation has been running down ever since—groaning and travailing in pain.

In other words, things are getting worse, not better. The evolutionary belief tells us that things have been improving—life has been evolving into more and more complex forms. For those Christians who believe in evolution, man should be improving—not getting worse. In fact, if Adam was part of an evolutionary progression, how could he fall upwards? What is sin? Is sin an inherited animal characteristic, or is it due to the fall of man through disobedience?

As scientists come to understand more of what is going on in this world, they find that our whole genetic make-up is degenerating. Mistakes in our genes are causing our physiology to have more and more problems.

3. NEW HEAVEN AND NEW EARTH

In Acts 3:21 (NIV) we read: "He must remain in heaven until the time comes for God to restore everything, as He promised long ago through His holy prophets." The Bible speaks of a time when this creation will be restored—that is, put back to what it used to be. This itself indicates that something is dreadfully wrong with today's world. For Christians who accept evolution, Paul's words about the whole of creation groaning and travailing in pain are meaningless.

The same is true when one speaks of the new heaven and new earth in which, as Scripture tells us, "righteousness dwells." Why is there need of a new heaven and new earth unless there is something wrong with the old one? Isaiah 11:6-9 (NIV) tells us what it will be like in the new heaven and the new earth:

"The wolf will live with the lamb, the leopard will lie down with the goat, the calf and the lion and the yearling together; and a little child will lead them. The cow will feed with the bear, the young will lie down together, and the lion will eat straw like the ox. The infant will play near the hole of the cobra, and the young child put his hand into the viper's nest. They will neither harm nor destroy on all my holy mountain, for the earth will be full of the knowledge of the Lord as the waters cover the sea." Here the description indicates that animals will not eat each other, but will eat plants (vegetarian)—and that there will be no violence or suffering.

Revelation 22:3 (NIV) tells us, "No longer will there by any curse." Revelation 21:4 (NIV) states: "He will wipe every tear from their eyes. There will be no more death or mourning or crying or pain, for the old order of things has passed away."

The description of what will happen in the restoration of all things can be summarized as follows: no death, no suffering, no bloodshed, no curse, vegetarian animals, no tears, no crying, no pain. This certainly is not a description of today's world—yet it is a description of a restoration, of something that reflects its former state.

When we read Genesis chapters 1 and 2, we find a description of the original creation—no death, no violence, animals vegetarian. In other words, this present creation will be restored to what it used to be because there is something dreadfully wrong with it at the moment. If a person accepts evolution, then what is the restoration going to be? Death, struggle and violence as we see today? Of course, this makes nonsense of the teachings of the new heaven and new earth given in Scripture.

4. ANIMALS CREATED TO BE VEGETARIAN

When we observe today's world, we notice that many animals eat other animals. Humans also eat the flesh of animals. The fact that we see violence among animals has been described by one poet as "nature red in tooth and claw." Evolutionists label the struggle as the "survival of the fittest." They see it as part of the evolutionary process. For theistic evolutionists, carnivorous (meat-eating) animals are just a part of this "creation" that God has supposedly used in the struggle towards man's evolution.

However, Genesis 1:29-30 (NIV) says: "Then God said, 'I Give you [Adam and Eve] every seed-bearing plant on the face of the whole earth and every tree that has fruit with seed in it. They will be yours for food. And to all the beasts of the earth and all the birds of the air and all the creatures that move on the ground—everything that has the breath of life in it—I give every green plant for food.' And it was so."

Man and animals were created to be vegetarian. This, of course, fits with the fact that there was no death before Adam's Fall. But, because of the entrance of sin into the world, death resulted. Sin affected the world so much that God caused a flood to come upon the earth in judgment. Genesis 6:12-13 (KJV) states: "And God looked upon the earth, and, behold it was corrupt; for all flesh had corrupted his way upon the earth. And God said unto Noah, The end of all flesh is come before me; for the earth is filled with violence through them; and, behold, I will destroy them with the earth." Part of this violence could have been animals starting to kill each other and perhaps man, and vice versa. Actually, though, man was not given specific instructions from God that he could eat meat until after Noah's Flood. Genesis 9:3 (NIV) tells us: "Everything that lives and moves will be food for you. Just as I gave you the green plants, I now give you everything."

Many people think that because animals have certain kinds of teeth they must have been created to be meat-eaters. However, there are many animals living today that have sharp canine teeth that eat only plants. Originally the teeth of these animals were used to eat the plants which God had made for them. As a result of the Fall, some animals now eat meat. Also, the Bible does not exclude the possibility of direct action by God at the time of the Fall having a direct biological effect on the creatures in relation to feeding habits.

5. CREATION IS FINISHED

The Bible teaches clearly that God finished His work of creating and making things on the sixth day of creation. "Thus the heavens and the earth were completed in all their vast array. By the seventh day God had finished the work He had been doing; so on the seventh day He rested from all His work. And God blessed the seventh day and made it holy. Because on it He rested from all the work of creation that He had done" (Genesis 2:1-3, NIV). God's work of creation finished at the end of the sixth day, when God completed all He had set out to do. However, because of man's fall God now works at reconciliation.

Those who believe that God used evolution must believe that the same processes God used in this supposed evolutionary "creation" are going on today. When the evolutionist looks at the world today, he observes mutations (mistakes or changes in genes) and natural selection (survival of the fittest) and sees these as part of the mechanisms of evolution. Given enough time, natural selection and mutations are said to enable organisms to change from one kind into another. What the evolutionist is doing, then, is using processes he observes today to extrapolate into the past. He believes these processes over millions of years are the basic mechanisms of evolution.

Christians who say God used evolution to bring everything including man into being have a real problem. If evolution is not occurring today (that is, if God is not "creating" through evolution), there is no basis to extrapolate into the past to say that evolution has ever occurred, as there is now no mechanism for it.

In other words, modern evolutionary theory accepts that evolution is still going on (therefore, man must still be evolving!), so if a Christian accepts evolution he has to accept that God is still using evolution today. Thus, He is still creating. But God tells us that He finished His work of creating. This is a real dilemma for the theistic evolutionist.

6. DUST TO ADAM—RIB TO EVE

We read in Genesis 2:7 (NIV) how God made the first man: "And the Lord God formed man from the dust of the ground and breathed into his nostrils the breath of life, and man became a living being."

According to this verse, taken at face value God made the first man Adam from the dust of the ground. His wife Eve was made in a different way. "So the Lord God caused the man to fall into a deep sleep; and while he was sleeping, He took one of the man's ribs and closed up the place with flesh. Then the Lord God made a woman from the rib He had taken out of the man, and He brought her to the man. The man said, 'This is now bone of my bones and flesh of my flesh; she shall be called "woman," because she was taken out of man'" (Genesis 2:21-23, NIV).

The first woman, Eve, was made from Adam's side. There are many Christians who, having accepted evolution, say that the "dust" in Genesis 2:7 actually represents the chemicals that God used to start the evolutionary process. Thus Genesis 2:7 represents a summary of evolution—that is, chemicals-to-man. Yet people who hold this belief have an insurmountable problem: if dust-to-Adam represents chemicals-to-man, then what does rib-to-Eve represent? To be consistent one needs an adequate explanation, and there is none—if one accepts evolution. Eve did not come directly from dust, but from an already fully functional created man.

7. RETURN TO DUST

Some people say the "dust" in Genesis 2:7 represents the animal (e.g., ape-like creature) that God breathed into and made into a man (Adam). They say that when the Bible tells us God took dust and made Adam, it is symbolic of the evolutionary understanding that ape-like creatures evolved into human beings. But again, one must be consistent. Genesis 3:19 (NIV) states, "By the sweat of your brow you will eat your food until you return to the ground, since from it you were taken; for dust you are and to dust you will return."

If the dust God used to make Adam represents an ape-like creature that God used to make man, then according to the Bible the dust from which man was made is what he returns to when he dies. To what **animal** does man return when he dies? Anyone can observe that when we die we return to dust—just as the Bible says. Dust of the ground, to which we return, is what we were created from in the first place!

8. GOD IS GOOD

In Genesis 1:31 (NIV) God pronounced of His creation that "it was very good." What did He mean by "good"? The only way you would know is if you had an absolute with which to make a comparison. Jesus said in Matthew 19:17 (KJV), "There is none good but one, that is, God." In Psalm 25:8 (NIV) we are told, "Good and upright is the Lord." Therefore, when God pronounced His creation as "good," what existed reflected the attributes of a God who is good. When we look at the attributes of God we see, for instance, as exhibited in the New Testament through Jesus Christ, that He cared for the sick, He healed the suffering, He raised the dead, He had compassion, He helped the weak. He is a loving and good God.

Now think about the methods of evolution: elimination of the weak, survival of the fittest, death and struggle in an evolutionary progression, elimination of the unfit, and so on. Would God have used this method in bringing all life into being and then describe it as **good**? Of course not—this would be totally inconsistent with God's nature as revealed in the Scriptures. Christians who believe that God used evolution must consider Him an ogre!

9. GENESIS IS LITERAL HISTORY

Many claim that Genesis is only symbolic—a kind of analogy. They claim it is not important what Genesis says, only what it **means.** Actually, it can't mean anything unless it says something anyway. Many Christians say that Genesis is meant only to teach us that God is Creator, but it is done in symbolic terms, because in reality the words really mean God used evolution.

However, if applying this idea—that Genesis is only symbolic—then one has to ask the question, "Where do we learn that God is Creator?" We can, of course, go to Genesis 1:1 (NIV) which says, "In the beginning God created the heavens and the earth." But if Genesis is only symbolic, to be consistent we would have to question whether the words "God created" are also symbolic. We would have to ask what this really means.

When people say Genesis is only symbolic, they are inconsistent, for they accept some parts as literal (such as "God created") and other parts as symbolic! If it is symbolic, then it must be written for a purpose, therefore, every phrase that is supposed to be symbolic must be a symbol of something. So one has to ask: What does every verse mean? What does it symbolize? For instance, what does "rib-to-Eve" symbolize? This makes no sense at all.[2] Either you take it at face value, or you

---

[2]It is, of course, powerfully symbolic (more correctly a **type**) of the future relationship between Christ and His church. But what does it tell us, symbolically or poetically or whatever, in its own context, about beginnings? Old Testament types (e.g., Moses as a type of Christ) are always real people and events in real history.

It is also important to note that the Jews divided their writings into three groups: history, poetry and prophecy. Genesis was included in their list of historical writings. Thus, they accepted it as real history.

don't know what it means, for it has no purpose being there.

10. ALL DOCTRINES FOUNDED IN GENESIS

Any basic study of Biblical doctrines of theology will show that ultimately all doctrines, directly or indirectly, have their basis in the book of Genesis.

In John 5:46-47 (NIV) Jesus Christ said: "If you believed Moses, you would believe me, for he wrote about me. But since you do not believe what he wrote, how are you going to believe what I say?" Jesus was emphatic that the writings of Moses had to be accepted to understand what He was saying because all the doctrines He taught were founded in Genesis. For instance, in Matthew 19:4-6 (NIV) we read of His answer to the question about divorce that concerned marriage: "Haven't you read, he replied, that at the beginning the Creator 'made them male and female' and said, 'For this reason a man will leave his father and mother and be united to his wife, and the two will become one flesh'? So they are no longer two, but one. Therefore what God has joined together, let not man separate."

Marriage has its foundation in Genesis—the first marriage God ordained is of Adam and Eve. To understand the meaning of marriage one must understand and accept its literal basis and origin as contained in the book of Genesis.

Christ died on a cross because of sin and death and the necessary shedding of blood for the remission of sins. The origin and basis of this is in the book of Genesis. We wear clothing because God gave clothes because of sin. We read this in the book of Genesis. To understand Christian doctrine we must understand the foundations of doctrine given in the book of Genesis. If Genesis cannot be taken literally, there is no foundation for Christian doctrine—therefore, Christian doctrine no longer has meaning.

Many people try to say that in the New Testament Jesus was only quoting the writings of His day—that He did not believe Genesis to be literal. They say that because the Jews happened to believe in the writings of Moses and in Genesis, Jesus just quoted this to go along with them. However, the Bible also teaches us that Jesus Christ is "the way, the truth and the life" (John 14:6). Jesus is the **truth**. To say that Jesus would knowingly teach "myth" as fact is to call Jesus Christ a liar. Jesus Christ was not just a man; He was not a sinner; He was the perfect "God-Man." Christians who say that Jesus was only quoting the myths of the day should be careful not to be calling Jesus a liar.

There are other instances where Jesus quoted from, or referred to, and thus accepted Genesis. For example, Matthew 24:37-39 (NIV): "As it was in the days of Noah, so it will be at the coming of the Son of Man. For in the days of the Flood, people were eating and drinking, marrying and giving in marriage, up to the day Noah entered the ark; and they knew nothing about what would happen until the Flood came and took them all away. That is how it will be at the coming of the Son of Man."

11. NEW TESTAMENT REFERENCES TO GENESIS

There are many references throughout the New Testament to Genesis, accepting it as literal history—as truth. There are at least 165 passages in Genesis that are either directly quoted or clearly referred to throughout the New Testament. Included in these are more than 100 quotations or direct references to Genesis chapters 1 through 11.

Every one of the New Testament authors refers in his writings to Genesis 1 through 11. Every one of the first 11 chapters is alluded to in certain sections throughout the New Testament. A complete listing of all New Testament references to Genesis can be found in Dr. Henry Morris' excellent commentary on Genesis, *The Genesis Record*, co-published by Baker Book House and Creation Life Publishers.

Throughout the Old and New Testaments Genesis is quoted from or referred to more than any other book in the entire Bible. This certainly indicates something of its importance. It also shows that both Old Testament and New Testament writers accepted Genesis as truth. On at least six occasions, Jesus Christ either quoted from or referred to some aspect of Genesis 1 through 11.

12. "DAYS" CANNOT BE "MILLIONS OF YEARS"

Many Christians claim that the days of creation actually represent millions of years of earth's history. They say that God did not create the universe in six literal days but in six periods of time, representing the millions of years held by the evolutionists.

First of all, one has to recognize that science cannot prove the age of the earth. There are many assumptions behind all of the dating methods of which most people are not aware. There is also much scientific evidence consistent with a belief in a young earth. But the Bible itself teaches quite clearly that the days in Genesis are ordinary, literal days (approximately 24 hours).

The Hebrew word for day, **yom**, can mean an ordinary day or an indefinite period of time. It should be made clear that the word for day in Genesis can never mean a long period in the definite sense. It can mean something longer than a day, but only in the indefinite sense (e.g., in the time of the Judges, in the day of the Lord). Exodus 20:11 tells us that God created the universe in six days and rested on one as a pattern for man. This is the reason God took as long as six days to make everything. He set the seven-day week pattern for us, which we still use today. God did not say He worked for six million years and rested for one million years, telling us to do the same. It makes even less sense to suggest he worked for six indefinite periods of time.

There are many other aspects at which we could look to show that the days must be ordinary days. For example, Adam was created on day six. He lived through day six, and day seven, and died when he was 930 years old. If each day were a million years, there are big problems here, too. It also needs to be made clear that the passage in II Peter 3:8, that compares a day to a thousand years is not defining the word "day" as a thousand years. In fact, taken in context II Peter 3:8 has nothing to do with the days of creation, but with the fact that God is outside time.

The word "day" when first used in Genesis cannot be symbolic. A word cannot be used symbolically the first time it is used. It can only be used symbolically when it first has a defined literal meaning. It is given this defined literal meaning in Genesis chapter 1 the first time it is used. Also, the words used for "evening" and "morning" can only mean exactly that.

In Genesis 1:14-19, concerning the fourth day of creation, the word "day" is used five times in relations to days, nights, seasons and years. If the word "day" here doesn't mean an ordinary day, it makes absolute nonsense of the way it is used in these passages.

13. AFTER HIS KIND

In Genesis 1, the phrase "after his kind" or "after their kind" occurs a total of ten times. This phrase is used in reference to the animals and plants as they are to reproduce on the earth. The Bible clearly teaches that God created fixed kinds of animals and plants, each to reproduce after its own kind. One kind could not change into another kind. Today we know there can be great variation within a kind, but fixed boundaries do exist. In fact, the classification system we use in naming animals and plants in groups was first formulated on the Biblical teaching of fixity of kinds, basically as the result of the work of Carl Linnaeus (1707-1778).

There is no indisputable in-between, transitional forms anywhere in the world, living or fossil. What we observe are distinct groups of animals and plants, as we would expect on the basis of what the Bible teaches. Those who believe in evolution have to make up additional theories as to why these in-between organisms are missing (e.g., "we haven't found them yet," or "evolution happened so fast that it left no in-between forms").

14. EVOLUTION AND GENESIS HAVE A DIFFERENT SEQUENCE

For those who try to harmonize evolution with Genesis, the order of evolution must compare with the order of events in Genesis. There are a number of problems here. The basic tenets of evolution totally conflict with the order in Genesis. For instance, Genesis teaches that God created fruit trees before fish—plants on day three, fish on day five. Evolution teaches that fish came before fruit trees. Evolution teaches that first life began in the sea, and after millions of years life was established on the land. The Bible teaches that the earth was first created covered with water: evolutionary teaching is that the earth first began as a hot molten blob. There is no way that the order of events according to evolution and Genesis can be reconciled.

15. THE EARTH CAME FIRST, NOT THE SUN

One evolutionary view of the earth's beginning is that, 20 billion years ago a Big Bang occurred, which resulted eventually in the sun forming and, subsequently, the earth as a hot molten blob. The Bible teaches that when God first created the heavens and the earth there was no sun. Light was created on the first day, but the sun was to act as the light-holder and was not made until day four. Also, the earth was covered with water when it was first made. In II Peter 3:5-6 we have a prophecy concerning the last days in which Peter tells us that men will deliberately choose to forget that the earth was created covered with water. The Big Bang theory and the Biblical account of creation are in total conflict.

16. GENESIS 1 AND 2—COMPLEMENTARY NOT CONTRADICTORY

Since Moses was not an eyewitness to creation, Noah's Flood or the events of the Tower of Babel, etc., presumably Genesis was a series of earlier records which Moses brought together in one publication under the direction of the Holy Spirit.

Because of the reference in the New Testament by Jesus to Moses and his authorship of the Pentateuch, there is very strong evidence to suggest that Moses was responsible for the book of Genesis. Throughout Genesis the phrase, "These are the generations of . . . " (e.g., Genesis 2:4), occurs a number of times. From external evidence, such as the use of what is called the colophon system in Mesopotamia, linguists say that these link passages ("these are the generations of") actually end each section. In other words, they are a kind of "signature" to most of the sections. Thus, in Genesis chapters 1 and 2 the first section goes from 1:1 to 2:4a, and the second section goes from 2:4b to 5:1a.

Many people say that Genesis chapter 1 and Genesis chapter 2 are two contradictory accounts of creation. In reality, it is easy to see that these two accounts of creation are not contradictory but complementary. Genesis 1:1 to 2:4a is an account in chronological order (first, second, third, etc.) of the days of creation. Genesis 2:4b begins the second account, which is a more detailed coverage of certain aspects of Genesis chapter 1. This second account is not meant to be chronological of each day of creation. In fact, it is meant to give a lot more of the details—particularly in relation to man and the garden—setting the scene for the fall of man in Genesis chapter 3.

The second account is extremely necessary for us to understand what happened in Genesis chapter 3. Not only that, the second account includes the actual details as to how God made man and woman, enabling us to understand more about the nature of the marriage relationship. The pattern of placing a more general account before the recording of certain specific events is not confined to the first two chapters of Genesis. We find it again in Genesis 10:2-32 where we have a population distribution table. This is followed by Genesis 11:1-10, which tells us what happened at Babel in about the third generation of the distribution genealogy in Genesis 10.

It should be noted that in Matthew 19:4-5, when Jesus replied concerning the question relating to marriage, He actually quoted from Genesis chapter 1 and Genesis chapter 2 in His reply, showing that He took them as complementary and authoritative. Matthew 19:4 (NIV) states: "Haven't you read, he replied, that at the beginning the Creator 'made them male and female" (Genesis 1:27). Matthew 19:5 (NIV): "And said, 'for this reason a man will leave his father and mother and be united to his wife, and the two will become one flesh'" (Genesis 2:24).

17. ADAM COULD WRITE

Those who believe in evolution speculate that as man evolved he first had to learn to grunt, then he had to learn to write. He had to use stone tools and learn about farming before he could develop what is called "advanced technology." However, the Bible tells us Adam was not "primitive" but a highly developed individual. For instance, we note in Genesis 2:20 (NIV) that "the man gave names to all the livestock, the birds of the air and all the beasts of the field." Adam could obviously speak; he had a complex language.

Further, in Genesis 3:20 (NIV) we are told that, "Adam named his wife Eve, because she would become the mother of all living." In Genesis 5:1 (NIV) we read that: "This is the written account of Adam's line."

Presumably, Adam wrote down all the details that God had given him concerning the original creation. He would have recorded the other events under God's direction, and Moses later obtained this material and compiled it into the book of Genesis. If this is so, then Noah must have taken on board the precious documents that Adam had written, in whatever form they existed.

It should also be noted that Adam's descendants made musical instruments and worked with brass and iron. Genesis 4:21-22 (NIV) states: "he was the father of all who play the harp and flute" and "Tubal-cain, who forged all kinds of tools out of bronze and iron . . . ." They were not primitive savages in the evolutionary progression.

18. NOAH'S FLOOD WORLD-WIDE, NOT LOCAL

Those Christians who accept the evolutionary view of earth's history believe that the billions of fossils found on earth are the result of processes occurring over millions of years. These processes are said to have involved the slow formation of sedimentary layers associated with the trapping of organisms and their subsequent fossilization. Therefore, when it comes to the section in Genesis chapters 6 through 9 concerning Noah's Flood, they have a problem. If there really was a world-wide flood, it would have ripped up this record from supposedly millions of years ago and destroyed it. On the other hand, the Bible teaches that there was no death before Adam sinned. Therefore, fossils couldn't have formed millions of years preceding Adam's sin.

However, there has to be an explanation for the millions of preserved animals and plants laid down by water in layers all over the earth. A world-wide flood such as that of Noah's time certainly is an excellent explanation. Christians who accept the fossil record as a result of millions of years of slow processes usually say Noah's Flood was only local in extent, not world-wide. The Bible teaches clearly that the water covered "all the high mountains under the entire heavens" (Genesis 7:19, NIV).

In addition, we are told in Genesis 9:11-13 of the covenant of the rainbow. God put a rainbow in the sky as a sign He would never again destroy the earth by a flood. We have obviously seen lots of floods since that time, but God has not broken His covenant, as He cannot do that. Therefore, these passages cannot be referring to a local event, but something which will never be repeated—a world-wide flood!

19. THEISTIC EVOLUTION EQUALS ATHEISTIC EVOLUTION PLUS GOD

In reality, theistic evolution is no different from atheistic evolution. God is simply added to the story. Christians who believe God used evolution accept what the atheistic view tells them, and then add God to the situation and reinterpret the Bible. Understanding the nature of man, that he is sinful and biased against God and that "there is none righteous, no not one," any view concerning the origin of life which has a consensus of opinion among non-Christians should at least be suspect. As the Bible is the Word of God—the God who knows everything, who has always been there, who does not tell a lie — everything we believe and think must be judged against God's Word. To understand any area of life we must have a Christian philosophy, which means we must start with the words of God, who was there, and not the words of men who were not.

20. ALL PEOPLE ARE DESCENDANTS OF ADAM

Because of their belief in evolution, there are Christians who consider that some of the cultures around the world are "primitive" in an evolutionary sense. They have not "evolved" as far as other cultures. However, the Bible teaches in I Corinthians 15:45 that Adam was the first man. There are not different races of men in an evolutionary sense. Romans 5:12 tells us that because of one man's sin (Adam) death passed upon all men, for all have sinned. All the different cultures of the world today have arisen since the time of the Tower of Babel. It was there that people began speaking different languages, causing them to go to different places on the earth's surface.

Every human being has the same ancestor, Adam, which is why we all have the same problem of sin and the same need for a Savior.

The same question the Lord asked the people of Israel through Joshua should be a stern reminder to us concerning whom we are choosing to believe. This passage states, "But if serving the Lord seems undesirable to you, then choose for yourself this day whom you will serve, whether the gods your forefathers served beyond the River, or the gods of the Amorites, in whose land you are living. But as for me and my household, we will serve the Lord" (Joshua 24:14, NIV).

Perhaps today we should ask ourselves a similar question. "Choose you this day whom you will believe: the words of men who are sinful creatures, who were not there, or the words of God who knows everything, who was there, and who has revealed to us all we need to know."

APPENDIX 2

WHY DID GOD TAKE SIX DAYS?

When one picks up a Bible, reads Genesis chapter 1 and takes it at face value, it seems to say that God created the world, the universe and everything in them in six ordinary (approximately 24-hour) days. However, there is a view in our churches which has become prevalent over the years that these "days" could have been thousands, millions or even billions of years in duration. Does it really matter what length these days were? Is it possible to determine whether or not they were ordinary days, or long periods of time?

WHAT IS A "DAY?"

The word for "day" in Genesis 1 is the Hebrew word "yom." It can mean either a day (in the ordinary 24-hour day), the daylight portion of an ordinary 24-hour day (i.e., day as distinct from the night), or occasionally it is used in the sense of an indefinite period of time (e.g., "In the time of the Judges" or "In the day of the Lord"). Without exception, in the Hebrew Old Testament the word "yom" never means "period" (i.e., it is never used to refer to a definite long period of time with specific beginning and end points). The word which means a long period of time in Hebrew is "olam." Furthermore, it is important to note that even when the word "yom" is used in the indefinite sense, it is clearly indicated by the context that the literal meaning of the word "day" is not intended.

Some people say the word "day" in Genesis may have been used symbolically and is thus not meant to be taken literally. However, an important point that many fail to consider is that a word can never be symbolic the first time it is used! In fact, a word can only be used symbolically when it has first had a literal meaning. In the New Testament we are told that Jesus is the "door." We know what this means because we know the word "door" means an entrance. Because we understand its literal meaning, it is able to be applied in a symbolic sense to Jesus Christ, so we understand that "He" is literally a door. The word "door" could not be used in this manner unless it first had the literal meaning we understand it to have. Thus, the word "day" cannot be used symbolically the first time it is used in the book of Genesis, as this is where God not only introduced the word "day" into the narrative, but also defined it as He invented it. Indeed, this is why the author of Genesis has gone to great lengths to carefully define the word "day" the first time it appears. In Genesis 1:4 (NIV) we read, "God called the light 'day,' and the darkness He called 'night.'" In other words, the terms were being very carefully defined. The first time the word "day" is used it is defined as "the light" to distinguish it from "the darkness" called "night." Genesis 1:5 (NIV) then finishes with: "And there was evening, and there was morning—the first day." This is the same phrase used for each of the other five days and shows there was a clearly established cycle of days and nights (i.e., periods of light and periods of darkness).

A DAY AND THE SUN

But how could there be day and night if the sun wasn't in existence? After all, it is clear from Genesis 1 that the sun was not created until day four. Genesis 1:3 tells us that God created light on the first day, and the phrase "evening and morning" shows there were alternating periods of light and darkness. Therefore, light was in existence, coming from one direction upon a rotating earth, resulting in the day and night cycle. However, we are not told exactly where this light came from. The word for "light" in Genesis 1:3 means the substance of light that was created. Then, on day four in Genesis 1:14-19 we are told of the creation of the sun which was to be the source of light from that time onward.

The sun was created to rule the day that already existed. The day stayed the same. It merely had a new light source. The first three days of creation (before the sun) were the same type of days as the three days with the sun.

Perhaps God deliberately left the creation of the sun until the fourth day because He knew that down through the ages cultures would try to worship the sun as the source of life. Not only this, modern theories tell us the sun came before the earth. God is showing us that He made the earth and light to start with, that He can sustain it with its day and night cycle and that the sun was created on day four as a tool of His to be the bearer of light from that time.

Probably one of the major reasons people tend not to take the days of Genesis as ordinary days is because they believe that scientists have proved the earth to be billions of years old. But this is not true. There is no absolute age-dating method to determine how old the earth is. Besides this, there is much evidence consistent with a belief in a young age for the earth, perhaps only thousands of years.

Incidentally, those who say that a day could be millions of years must answer the question, "What is a night?"

WHY SIX DAYS?

God is an infinite being. This means He has infinite power, infinite knowledge, infinite wisdom. Obviously, God could then make anything He desired. He could have created the whole universe, the earth and all it contains in no time at all. Perhaps the question we should be asking is why did God take as long as six days? After all, six days is a peculiar period for an infinite being to make anything. The answer can be found in Exodus 20:11. Exodus 20 contains the Ten Commandments, and it should be remembered that these commandments were written on stone by the very "finger of God." In Exodus

we read: "When the Lord finished speaking to Moses on Mount Sinai, He gave him the two tablets of the Testimony, the tablets of stone inscribed by the finger of God" (Exodus 31:18, NIV). The fourth commandment in verse 9 of chapter 20 tells us that we are to work for six days and rest for one. The justification for this is given in verse 11: "For in six days the Lord made the heavens and the earth, the sea, and all that is in them, but He rested on the seventh day. Therefore the Lord blessed the Sabbath day and made it holy." This is a direct reference to God's creation week in Genesis 1. To be consistent (and we must be), whatever is used as the meaning of the word "day" in Genesis 1 must also be used here. If you are going to say the word "day" means a long period of time in Genesis, then it has been already shown that the only way this can be is in the sense of the "day" being an indefinite or indeterminate period of time, **not** a definite period of time. Thus the sense of Exodus 20:9-11 would have to be "six indefinite periods shalt thou labor and rest a seventh indefinite period." This, however, makes no sense at all. By accepting the days as ordinary days, we understand that God is telling us He worked for six ordinary days and rested one ordinary day to set a pattern for man—the pattern of our seven-day week which we still have today.

DAY-AGE INCONSISTENCIES

There are many inconsistencies in accepting the days in Genesis as long periods of time. For instance, we are told in Genesis 1:26-28 that God made the first man (Adam) on the sixth day. Adam lived through the rest of the sixth day and through the seventh day. We are told in Genesis 5:5 that he died when he was 930 years old. (We are not still in the seventh day as some people misconstrue, for Genesis 2:2 tells us God **"rested"** from His work of creation, not that He is **resting** from His work of creation.) If each day was, for example, a million years, then there are real problems. In fact, if each day were only a thousand years long, this still makes no sense of Adam's age at death either.

A DAY IS AS A THOUSAND YEARS

But some then refer to II Peter 3:8 (NIV) which tells us: "With the Lord a day is like a thousand years, and a thousand years are like a day." This verse is used by many who teach, by inference at least, that the days in Genesis must each be a thousand years long. This reasoning, however, is quite wrong. Turning to Psalm 90:4 (NIV), we read a similar verse: "For a thousand years in your sight are like a day that has just gone by, all like a watch in the night." In both II Peter 3 and Psalm 90 the whole context is that God is neither limited by natural processes nor by time. To the contrary, God is "outside" time, for He also "created " time. Neither verse refers to the days of creation in Genesis, for they are dealing with God not being bound by time. In II Peter 3, the context is in relation to Christ's second coming, pointing out the fact that with God a day is just like a thousand years or a thousand years is just like one day. He is outside of time. This has nothing to do with the days of creation in Genesis.

Further, in II Peter 3:8 the word "day" is contrasted with "a thousand years." The word "day" thus has a literal meaning which enables it to be contrasted with "a thousand years." It could not be contrasted with "a thousand years" if it didn't have a literal meaning. Thus, the thrust of the Apostle's message is that God can do in a very short time what men or "nature" would require a very long time to accomplish, if they could accomplish it at all. It is interesting to note that evolutionists try to make out that the chance, random processes of "nature" required millions of years to produce man. Many Christians have accepted these millions of years, added them to the Bible and then said that God took millions of years to make everything. However, the point of II Peter 3:8 is that God is not limited by time, whereas evolution requires time (a very great deal of it!).

DAYS AND YEARS

In Genesis 1:14 (NIV) we read that God said, "Let there be lights in the expanse of the sky to separate the day from the night, and let them serve as signs to mark seasons and days and years." If the word "day" here i' not a literal day, then the word "years" being used in the same ver'   ·1 be meaningless.

DAY AND COVENANT

Turning to Jeremiah 33:25-26 (NIV) we read: "This is what the Lord says: 'If I have not established my covenant with day and night and fixed laws of heaven and earth, then I will reject the descendants of Jacob, and David my servant and will not choose one of his sons to rule over the descendants of Abraham, Isaac and Jacob. For I will restore their fortunes and have compassion on them.'" The Lord is telling Jeremiah that He has a covenant with the day and the night which cannot be broken, and it is related to the promise to the descendants of David, including the One who was promised to take the throne (Christ). This covenant between God and the day and night began in Genesis 1, for God first defined and invented day and night when He spoke them into existence. There is no clear origin for day and night in the Scripture other than Genesis 1. Therefore, this must be the beginning of this covenant. So if this covenant between the day and the night does not exist when God clearly says it does (i.e., if you do not take Genesis 1 to literally mean six ordinary days), then this promise given here through Jeremiah is on shaky ground.

DOES THE LENGTH OF THE DAY MATTER?

Finally, does it really matter whether we accept them as ordinary days or not? The answer is a most definite "Yes!" It is really a principle of how one approaches the Bible. For instance, if we don't accept them as ordinary days then we have to ask the question, "What are they?" The answer is "We don't know." If we approach the days in this manner, then to be consistent we should approach other passages of Genesis in the same way. For instance, when it says God took dust and made Adam—what does this mean? If it does not mean what is says, then we don't know what it means! We should take Genesis literally. Furthermore, it should be noted that you cannot "interpret literally," for a "literal interpretation" is a contradiction in terms. You either take it literally or you interpret it! It is important to realize we should take it literally unless it is obviously symbolic, and when it is symbolic either the context will make it quite clear or we will be told in the text.

If a person says that we do not know what the word "day" means in Genesis, can another person who says they are literal days be accused of being wrong? The answer is "No," because the person who accepts them as ordinary days does know what they mean. It is the person who does not know what the days mean who cannot accuse anyone of being wrong.

People try to make the word "day" say something else because they are trying to make room for the long ages of evolutionary geology. This doesn't work because these supposed ages are represented by fossils showing death and struggle, and thus you are left with the same old problem of death and struggle before Adam.

When people accept at face value what Genesis is teaching and accept the days as ordinary days, they will have no problem understanding what the rest of Genesis is all about.

For in six days the Lord made the heavens and the earth, the sea, and all that is in them, but He rested on the seventh day. Therefore the Lord blessed the Sabbath day and made it holy" (Exodus 20:11, NIV).

INDEX OF MAJOR
REFERENCES

A Great Companion Book!

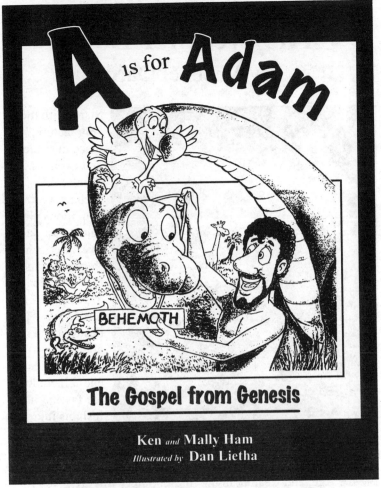

A is for Adam

BEHEMOTH

The Gospel from Genesis

Ken *and* Mally Ham
Illustrated by Dan Lietha

A Genesis Commentary for Parents and Children

A Three-in-one Multipurpose Family Book!
➤ Entertaining ABC Rhyme Book
➤ Devotional Teaching Book for Sunday School, Christian School, Home School, and Family Devotions
➤ Coloring Book

The Weather Book
by Michael Oard

Starts with the "big picture," our place in space, and explains how each of the various weather conditions play a role in our daily lives. Learn how thunderstorms build, hurricanes are formed, tornadoes destroy, and about crazy weather phenomenon. Included are fascinating insights into weather of the past, including Noah's flood and the Ice Age, and weather in the future. Safety tips are given for dangerous situations and instructions for building a weather station. First in an exciting creation science series honoring God as Creator. Future topics in the series include geology, biology, astronomy, archaeology, and oceanography. The quality of design, artwork, and information will make learning a joy! Spectacular inside color illustrations dominate every page. Interest level: 4th grade - adult.

ISBN: 0-89051-211-6
Hardcover • 8-1/2 x 11 • $15.95

Available at Christian bookstores nationwide.

══ *Answers in Genesis* ══
Video Series
with Ken Ham and Gary Parker

Filmed at an *Answers in Genesis* seminar, this series features the most popular presentations by Ken Ham and Gary Parker. Professionally produced, with outstanding visuals, this series is ideal for Sunday school, mini-seminars, home use or outreach.

Tapes include these topics:
- What Really Happened to the Dinosaurs? - *Ham*
- Dinosaurs and the Bible - *Parker*
- A Walk through Genesis (Part 1 and 2) - *Ham*
- Life Before Birth - *Parker*
- Genesis and the Decay of the Nations (Parts 1 and 2) - *Ham*
- From Evolution to Creation - *Parker*
- Facts and Bias - *Ham*
- Genes and Genesis - *Parker*
- Creation Evangelism - *Ham*
- Fossils and the Flood - *Parker*

A powerful evangelism and training video program helping Christians reach this generation for Christ!

Master Books
P.O. Box 727
Green Forest, AR 72638

In the Days of Noah
by Gloria Clanin and
Earl and Bonnie Snellenberger

The historical event known as the Great Flood of Noah so devastated the earth's surface that the ancient world has been lost to us. But this spectacular new book gives a wide-eyed look into what life must have been like 5,000 years ago. Drawing from information in the Bible, *In the Days of Noah* paints a breath-taking view of God's judgment on a sinful world. The detail in each color illustration is so striking, young and older readers alike will gain remarkable insight into antediluvian life. Basic questions such as ship size, care of the animals, and many others are answered. A Bible story wrapped in a gorgeous picture book, this work is unique in the publishing world. Interest level: 4th grade - adult.

ISBN: 0-89051-205-1
Hardcover • 8-1/2 x 11 • $14.95

Available at Christian bookstores nationwide.